Memoirs of Miracles

CONTENTS

1	The Early Years	1
2	Years of Preparation	45
3	Ministry in Japan	55
4	Our Ministry in the U.S.	135
5	Retirement	207

Preface

During our 66 years of happy married life, we have witnessed many miracles, but we've had to acknowledge that one cannot experience a miracle without first experiencing a trial. Also we have realized it is not always our weak faith that produces miracles, for often we are most surprised at our answers. Just like the disciples, while they were praying for Peter's release from prison, they would not believe Rhoda when she excitedly announced that he was standing at the gate. They said, "You are mad. It is his angel." All that happened in our lives, our trials and miracles, we attribute to an all-wise and loving God as we have set our hearts to love and follow Him.

If anyone can profit from our history —some humorous, some tragic, but always with miracles, though not perceived at the time – we would be greatly humbled. Please remember, if you are not a Christian, there is a loving God who is seeking and longing for your fellowship. That's why He gave His Son to die on the cross for your sins, to rise again, and is now seated at the right hand of the Father, waiting for you to give your requests to Him. Please open your heart's door and receive His precious gift of eternal life.

Bernie & Jeanette Holritz

Chapter One
Early Year: 1921 ~ 1945

JEANNETTE'S STORY

Birth and Early years

I, Dora Jeanette Miller, made my entrance into this world on July 30, 1925. My earliest memory is that my little brother, two years

younger than I, had fun together. But there were times when I would purposely lead him into trouble. One of my mother's "no-noes" was not to crawl under our beds. When he was old enough to crawl, I would say, "Earl, Mother is not watching – let's go!" Then I would scramble out and holler at mother saying, "Earl's under the bed," leaving him in trouble. So you see, I was an imp from the time I was born. Another time, I talked Earl into saving our Milky Way candy bars which had been given to us earlier.

Early Years

We snuck them into our bed with the idea of seeing who could make our Milky Way last the longest. I was the loser that time! Earl had eaten his neatly, but I fell asleep eating mine, so the next morning my hair was turned into a beautiful "mop" gummed with Milky Way! Naturally, I was the one in trouble.

I remember the night my younger sister was born on the kitchen table, and I marveled at her first cry from my bedroom. All this happened in a home that was called, "The Old Seaton Farm." It was in a totally remote country setting. As I remember, there was not a single neighbor around, and an aura of mystery seemed to hover over the place. Added to the mystery was that my daddy would point to an old gnarled tree with one branch which seemed to say, "I'm here for a purpose." What made it even scarier is that my daddy would say, "That's were the Niggers were hanged!" It was hard for me to believe these stories as this was between 1925 and 1930 -- sixty years after the Emancipation Proclamation. However, my daddy was a member of the Ku Klux Klan!

After Seaton Place

After Seaton Place, we moved to another house. It was at this house I have the most dominant picture of my mother lying on the floor after having been knocked down by my daddy who had come home at 3 a.m. after a night with one of his girl friends.

But the most tragic of all my memories took place in still another house. I'll never forget when my mother sat across the table from a neighbor lady and explained that she was two months pregnant, and felt it was too much for her as my little sister was only eleven months old. The neighbor advised her to take a crayon and push it up into the fetus, which she did. The result was my mother was rushed to the hospital and wasn't expected to live. (I have always blamed my daddy for this event, but I still do not believe my mother should have performed a self-afflicted abortion. I think my mother should have left my daddy long before after he had so brutally abused her.)

The day came when they knew she was dying. There was a crowd standing outside the hospital when someone announced, "She is gone!" When I heard that, I screamed, "Oh no!" I was just nine years old. It seems strange that no one sought to comfort us children neither at that time nor at the funeral, though someone must have been caring for my baby sister. But God performed a miracle, which I will never forget, though it meant more to me later than it did at the time. As I was milling around listening to the people talk, I heard one lady say, "Isn't it a shame that she died leaving all those children," (there were five of us) to which the other lady replied, "But haven't you heard? Brother South talked to her yesterday and she accepted Jesus as her Savior." A couple of years later, after I became a Christian, I asked who Brother South was and they replied, "He is a Baptist preacher in your mother's home town." In fact, he took part in my mother's funeral though I didn't realize it at the time.

Something happened shortly after my mother's funeral that pierced my heart like an arrow. My father took the phone outside the room in which I was sitting and I realized he was talking to one of his girl friends and asking her for a date. My daddy said, "We don't have to worry about her. She's dead!"

Then we moved to a place that was called "a shotgun house" built on blocks. These little houses were built in a row with only a few feet between. We were left alone each night. One night when our neighbor drove up to his place, the lights from the car revealed a black man under our house! There were a few other happenings such as one of daddy's buddies tried to attack me, but I escaped from him.

I was still only nine years of age when I was to assume a new role. I don't know how we would have survived if I didn't cook, we could not have eaten; or if I didn't wash and iron, we wouldn't have had any clean clothes. This was under the most strenuous conditions: no washing machine, no bathtub, and an old kerosene stove. The iron was heated on the stove hoping it would be the right temperature so that I wouldn't scorch my daddy's starched white shirts. I don't believe I could have stepped into my role as housekeeper if I hadn't spent summers with my Grandmother Miller between the ages of six and eight. Grandma absolutely loathed lazy girls and let it be known. Her mother had been bedridden and she, of necessity, had to do the housekeeping. So as it was with mother and daughter, it would be with grandmother and granddaughter. I loved my grandmother and followed her around like a little puppy dog. If she was outside, I was with her scrubbing the clothes, as she stoked the fire under the huge iron cauldron. I was also with her feeding the chickens or tilling the garden, and then I would follow her to the kitchen for making goodies.

I took my responsibilities seriously, and I don't ever remember that I disliked my job. Maybe I liked being the boss of my siblings! Instead all my sisters seemed to love me, and my youngest sister still calls me "Mama Sister." I remember one of my sisters laughingly asked me, "Do you remember chasing me down the block because I didn't want my hair washed?" Oh the blessing of being a young "mother!" Recently one of my sisters reminded me how I used to make up fairy tales and tell them at night before they all went to sleep. She said, "I remembered vividly a part of one of the stories and I was wondering if I could tell her the rest!"

Then something happened which could have been a tragedy, but turned out to be my greatest miracle. I was cooking with a heavy skillet filled with oil when it suddenly caught fire. I foolishly picked it up, dropped it, and was pinned behind the flames. One of my younger sisters remembers me running out the front door screaming. My brother called the neighbors who in turn called

Chapter 1

the ambulance. Thankfully, I only had surface burns on one side of my body. Some ladies from a nearby church read or heard about my accident, and while I was at home in bed they brought me the most delicious meal I had ever eaten. They also invited me to their church.

Later I was reminded of the two ladies, their kindness and invitation to visit their church. The Sunday I went, they were having an evangelistic meeting. I learned that Jesus died for my sins. On my tenth birthday, a fourteen-year old girl said, "Let's go to the store and get you some presents." I thought she would buy them for me, but when she saw something, she would ask me if I liked it and then said, "Put it in your pocket!" I knew that I was a sinner, not only from this incident, but others as well. When they were singing, "There Is a Fountain Filled With Blood" I went forward to accept Jesus as my Savior. Oh the joy that flooded my heart until I looked down at my dress provided by the relief, I noticed that the hem was out! My first thought was that I shouldn't have gone down before all those people. But then I changed my mind, "I don't care. I'm so happy," and skipped all the way home and told my brother, but I was too afraid to tell my daddy.

Then my stepmother joined us in the shotgun house. One day my father announced, "Jeanette, I want you and Earl to kill the old red rooster, (penned in a cage under the house) and have chicken and dumplings ready for supper when we get back from visiting mother's folks." Earl and I looked at each other quizzically and I said, "If that rooster is killed, you'll have to do it. I can do the rest." (Neither of us knew how to wring its neck like my grandmother used to do.) With that Earl found an axe, and while I held this stubbornly resistant creature's feet, Earl accomplished the act! Fortunately, my grandmother had taught me how to scald a chicken, pluck its feathers (p u!) and cut it up properly for boiling. I was eleven, Earl was nine, but by the time our parents returned in the evening, the meal with all its trimmings was ready to serve. Mission accomplished!

School Days

I will give the only other picture I have of my mother sitting in a rocker, with me on her lap, teaching me to read and later at the table learning to write and do some basic arithmetic. Our school system had what was called "Primary" followed by eleven grades to graduate from high school. Because of my mother's teaching, I was told I could skip "Primary" and enter first grade. That would mean I could graduate from high school in eleven years at the age of 17, if I finished the course.

Some people have asked me, "Between the time that my mother died, and my father remarried, what my siblings would do while I was in school?" I honestly cannot answer that question. The only thing I remember is one day when I came home from school; there were two women in my bed, up to no good.

My father, who was a contractor and painter, built us a modest house across the street from the old shotgun house. While we were living in that house, a man of whom we were deathly afraid, would stop by, usually during the day. One day, my stepmother asked me to go to that man's house to help his wife with some chores. I was afraid, but I thought I had better obey. Thankfully, the husband was not at home. The day after I had been at that house, he murdered his wife and five children!

If I thought my home chores were to be lightened a great deal because I had a stepmother, I was totally wrong. My father saw to that. (He did not believe a girl should be educated beyond grade school.) A woman was simply a toy for a man. So I resumed my duties as expected. That included rising before the rest of the family, starting the old wood-stove, making breakfast, and doing the dishes. If I finished all that, I could go to school,

Chapter 1

for which I fought. But that was not all. When I got home, there were babies to tend (which came quite often). However, this was the part I liked most. There were other household chores and if they were done, and everyone else was in bed, I was free to study. It was awful when I would have to stay an hour late in the library in order to finish a project. I knew what to expect! My daddy would meet me at the door, beat me, and accuse me of lying out with some boy. Nevertheless, at seventeen, I graduated from high school with honors. Of the thirteen siblings, I was one of only two to graduate.

My Two Grandparents

Can two grandmothers brought together by marriage into one family be so opposite in every way? I think not. However, realism proved me wrong.

I told you a little about my Grandmother Miller, but now I want to introduce you to my maternal Grandmother Baxter. She was wealthy in houses and lands, a sizable bank account, and servants, with prospects of oil on her land and a fortune in sight, through her mother, if all went well with their executor in NY. Now I want to tell you there are Millers on both sides of the family. Apparently Great Grandmother Miller was the source of all the wealth. Unfortunately the executor appeared at the Baxter home and Great Grandmother Miller refused to see him. He was so angry he sought out someone else in the family – namely my daddy. Because my daddy befriended him, he told him, "As soon as I return to NY I will see that you receive the fortune and you will never have to lack for anything the rest of your life." But he died the day after he arrived in NY. I have never heard whether the Baxters received their due inheritance.

My Grandmother Baxter wasn't well with a disease called Pellagra, caused by a lack of niacin. The only way it seemed to affect her is that her skin was ghostly white. Though she was not a Christian – in fact on her mother's side all claimed to be atheists -- yet I will have to say, I have never met a more moral woman. One day a grandson and granddaughter were acting improperly with each other's bodies, and she came to me crying. I told her, "Kids sometime do things like that, but if they are taught well, they will turn out alright."

As I said, Grandma Baxter wasn't a Christian. When I wanted to listen to "The Old Fashioned Revival Hour," she objected – her reason being she didn't like the voice of "Honey", Dr. Fuller's wife. Unlike my Grandma Miller, she never taught me anything

in the kitchen. She did teach me to embroidery, and I made several acceptable dresser scarves that we later used in our own home. One of the joys I experienced living at the Baxter's home was with my mother's sister who had been living with my grandmother since her divorce. Aunt Evelyn, whom I stayed with when I visited, was a jovial person, so we had fun together, and I'm afraid she had to put up with my foolishness.

Chapter 1

I must confess, now that Aunt Evelyn is in the picture, I remember I have one more episode to relate. Mother and Aunt Evelyn were driving in the car and I was in the backseat. They were discussing some of their lady friends when Aunt Evelyn asked if she were "eggapra?" I chuckled within myself that they would think that at 7, I was too young to know what they were talking about. I loved adult conversation and I rarely missed anything they said. Of course, the word "pregnant" was not used loosely in those days, and especially within a child's hearing.

Now I must tell you about Grandma Baxter's attic of which we five siblings were terrified. To add to our fright, grandpa's brother, Uncle Jim, a short shriveled up old man who looked like a wind would blow him away, lived up there. He rarely came downstairs, but once we had seen him, we hid our faces. It seems strange now, but when I was a teenager and Uncle Jim was gone, grandma said we should go to the attic. I followed her upstairs with trepidation. But what I found was amazing. There were lots of windows, and sunshine flooded the place. I wondered why I was ever afraid of the attic. Grandma showed me some interesting mementoes of things past, plus her old wax doll which would have melted if held too close to the fireplace. Before Grandma Baxter died she specified in her will that the part due to our mother would be passed on to the five of us. (When our mother died, Grandma Baxter tried to adopt us, but was unsuccessful. In retrospect, I wish this would have happened as it would have spared my younger sister from being sexually abused by my father.) When the time came to receive the inheritance, my father flew into a rage saying, "That money belonged to me!" In order to quiet him, we each gave him some money.

As for Grandpa Baxter, all I remember of him was his face and his quietness. Was it because he was a farm boy, or was it because grandma had all the money? However, I do not ever remember hearing a cross word between them. Before I leave the Baxters, we were all saddened with the news that my Aunt Evelyn had cancer. After our marriage, Bernie and I made several visits to see her. On one of our visits, she made it clear that she wanted to become a Christian. What a changed person! What a miracle!

I have already told you my Grandma Baxter was rich and Grandma Miller was poor, but the Millers never lacked for nourishing food. They were sufficient with chickens, garden, and a few animals. I loved the farm atmosphere as well as sleeping under those cozy feather bed comforters. (Grandma said the feathers would protect me from lightening.) There was also the nostalgic sound of the train that passed behind the house at exactly 3 a.m. every morning – whistle and all. I remember my Grandma Miller as an industrious woman and patient to teach. But my sweetest memory is of her sitting in the rocker reading her Bible. I believe it was my Grandmother Miller that instilled in me the love of the Word of God. After grandpa died, I would sleep in the bed next to her. She would ask me to read the Bible to her. Later she would waken and say, "Child, are you still reading?"

Grandma had good ears. She would put newspapers on the bottom of her dresser drawers. In the night, she would get up, turn on the light, and I would ask her what she was doing. She would say, "I heard a roach crawling in one of the drawers and I'm going to get him." Unlike my home, neither of my grandmas' houses had roaches. In my home, I would cover my head in order to keep those big pests from attacking my face.

The most tragic picture of my Grandma Miller was when her legs gave way while climbing the stairs of her back porch. I was alone with grandma. When I got help, she was taken to the hospital where she was fitted with a body cast from her neck to her feet. A large stick was part of the cast that would allow her to be lifted. She was to lie in this "new dress" for three hot summer months with no air conditioning. Her doctor said, "You'll never walk again," but she said emphatically, "<u>I will</u>." When her cast was taken off, she was left with atrophy of the body, unable to move. I asked my cousin, who was a surgical nurse, if they had physical therapy in those days, and she said, "No." But my grandma claimed she had prevented grandpa from a serious heart attack by massaging his chest. So perhaps she had an innate knowledge that would help get her body going. Eventfully she found she could put one foot on the floor and later the other. Then her secret began. While no one was in the room, she discovered she could stand, and from there learned to take a few steps. When she was able to walk, she called the others to observe. I can't ever remember her walking with a cane, and amazingly she stood as straight as an arrow.

Grandpa Miller was quiet, but a hard worker. I recall grandma and grandpa sitting by the kerosene lamp reading the Bible, but I can never forget when Aunt Donna's bull got loose and stalked grandpa until his faithful dog, Jack, chased him off so grandpa could climb a tree -- another "Lassie," another miracle!

Post High School Years

After high school, I went directly to one of President Roosevelt's projects, the National Youth Administration, teaching students

how to work on airplanes. (When later I told this to Paul, exclaimed, "Wow, Mom.") This qualified me to get a job at the Naval Airbase, but then they decided I would be a better typist than "Rosy the Riveter." I think my father knew that if I were hired at the Naval Base, I would receive a generous salary and could help out with the family expenses. I made nine dollars and twelve cents an hour that, at that time, was an unheard of wage for a teenage girl!

My daddy had a very serious accident in which the other driver was at fault so he was able to collect insurance that enabled him to build a second house on his property. Grandpa Miller had died and grandma needed a place to stay. I soon understood that my part was to live in that house with grandma, pay the rent, utilities, and purchase all the food. Then something happened which was difficult for me to believe. As I said earlier, I was making a good wage at the naval base, and thought nothing of it when I bought an old piano for fifty dollars as well as a violin to help my sisters gain some of the things I had been denied. As soon as I had the piano delivered, my daddy met me at the door, with belt in hand, threatening me. "Either that piano goes or you do!" I finally decided this was not a test God was putting on me, but my father was trying to snuff out my life. When I mentioned the situation to a lady I worked with at the base, she invited me to come, with my piano, and live with her and her daughter. The next day I called the mover and got settled in my new home.

Sometime later, I read about a famous Jewish evangelist, Dr. Nathan Cohen Beskin, who was to speak at a Nazarene church near my family's house, and I decided to go. Lo and behold, my daddy was sitting on the front row, Jekyll and Hyde that he was. Daddy invited Dr. Beskin to go to meet his mother. I don't know if my daddy was startled to see me or not, but as soon as he saw me, he invited me to come home WITH my piano! Naturally, I was glad to be with my siblings and grandma again. As I look back on this incident, I don't know what would have happened had I stayed with this lady as I could not have remained there indefinitely, and yet where could I have gone? I really needed to be in my own home and in my own area in order to meet the love of my life!

Early Years

Romance

On this particular evening, our youth group from Calvary Baptist Church, together with some sailors from the naval base, was holding a street meeting. One sailor took note of a young lady with a large Bible giving her testimony. At that point, he nudged the sailor next to him and said, "I'm going to marry that girl." Will he keep his word?

I had a dear older friend from the naval base, Gracie Howard, who invited me to help her with the youth group at the Methodist church she founded which met after the evening service. So when our Baptist church service was finished, I would slip over to her church. One day, Gracie asked me to take part in their first anniversary service which was to be on a Sunday afternoon.

In the meantime, a friend asked me to go to San Antonio with her and her family on that same afternoon. For the first time, my daddy had given me permission to go out of town. As much as I wanted to go, I quickly said, "No," as I had promised Gracie I would speak at their service. On that same Sunday afternoon, a group of sailors, as was their usual habit, were praying that God would guide them to a church where they could give their testimonies. One of the three had read in the newspaper that a Methodist church was having an anniversary meeting that afternoon. They decided that's where they would go. Sure enough, the floor was opened up for testimonies and the sailors each gave a word.

As soon as the service was over, a tall sailor came up to the platform where I was and introduced himself as Bernie Holritz. He said he had seen me at a street service some nights before. We talked about the Bible and our faith for about an hour. I thought how refreshing it was to converse with a young man who knew the Lord.

Soon after that Gracie said, "Jeanette, I want you to get on the phone and call that Bernie Holritz to speak to the youth next Sunday evening. And if I were you, I would set my cap for him." I replied, "Gracie, I can't do that as my grandma told me never to call a boy." But for the sake of the church, I acquiesced! On Sunday night Bernie spoke to the young people and my sister Jennie Lee was there and she was saved. After the meeting, Bernie walked us home and prayed with us.

Call to Missions

Sometime previous to this incident, I had an indescribable feeling as if God were trying to tell me something, but I didn't know what. I confided in a friend who was a secretary in a Baptist church. She told me I needed a closer walk with God, but she could not tell me how, nor answer my question about discerning the will of God. One day I took time off from work and went to a park to be alone. It seemed God was saying, "I want you to be a missionary." But now what!? At that time I was in a Southern Baptist church which had a "Lottie Moon Offering" once a year– a gift for missionaries. I attended that church for several years, but never saw a missionary nor heard a sermon on missions. Clearly that was not the place for me. But God was good and I received help when I changed to an independent Baptist church.

Now that these two have met, will they keep their interest up and will the young man keep his promise. To find out what happened, read Bernie's story which follows.

BERNIE'S STORY

Birth and early childhood

On a routine examination, when my mother was six months pregnant, Dr. Lorenzen, our family doctor, discovered a large tumor in her abdomen! It would be a delicate procedure, endan-

Early Years

gering both her life and the baby's. He felt assured that he could save her life, but there was a real possibility that the child could not survive the ordeal. Surgery to remove the tumor was to be the next day! Mother spent the night in prayer asking the Lord to spare both her life and the baby's, and promised the Lord if He would save the baby, she would dedicate the child to Him. I was that baby, and I made my appearance on October 25, 1921, at 7:30 in the morning. I was born at home, of course, as was every baby in those days, and Dr. Lorenzen delivered me. My mother did not tell me this story until after I was saved at the age of 19.

An interesting side light, at this point, regarding Dr. Lorenzen: he was a wonderful doctor who considered the people of Grant County as his "flock." Later that same year, he became quite famous for an act of heroism when he risked his life by riding his horse several miles through a blinding snowstorm to deliver a baby for a lady who was in hard labor. The papers covered the story nationwide.

North Dakota was not very densely populated at that time, and Carson had about 400 people. (I made it 401!) What sidewalks we had were made of wood. It was the county seat with the courthouse in the middle of town. There was a general merchandize store which also housed the post office, and a few other businesses all on the main street. We also had a church, but no local pastor. A Presbyterian circuit rider would hold services. From what my mother said, he was a very godly man with a wonderful singing voice, and dearly loved by the people.

I was the youngest of four children. My sister, Alta, was the oldest; thirteen years my senior; Adolph was 5 years younger, and Clarence was born 18 months later. I was "the caboose," arriving six and a half years after Clarence. As the youngest, I had a lot of TLC as well as playtime from each of my siblings. Another thing that encouraged attention was the fact that I was born with a digestive problem which caused much discomfort.

Chapter 1

I really don't remember very much about Carson. But when I was two and a half, I contracted diphtheria. There was one other child in the state that had it at the same time as I did. We were given a very potent drug and told not to move. So my mother held me for three days. The other boy was older than I and one day asked for a drink of water. He raised his head to drink and died a few moments later!

There are lots of stories about my brothers' exploits I remember from those early days, only because they were told so many times. There are two which I like the most. One was about my two brothers who were fussing about who had the most room in the bed. My mother had told them to quiet down and go to sleep, but they continued! She finally went upstairs, got them both out of bed; sent them out in the backyard to pick up a fence pole; bring it up to their bed, place it in the middle, and then get in, each on his own side! The next morning they were busy pulling slivers out of each other. They never argued about that again!

Another story is about some "target practicing." The two boys who lived across the street from us were good friends of my two brothers. Between the four of them, it was pretty hard to stay out of trouble. The father of the other two boys was the car dealer for the town, and he had just received a shipment of new model cars and stored them in a warehouse waiting their "unveiling." The circus was soon coming to town and they had plastered one side of the warehouse with their usual animal pictures. One day, the boys across the street decided they would try to shoot the eyes out of the animals! They had a high powered rifle which my brothers were afraid to try because of the "kick" of the rifle. What they didn't realize was the bullets not only went through the wood of the shed, but also through the windshields and bodies of the cars stored in the warehouse! My brothers were glad they had not participated in the target practice.

My father had been county auditor for twelve years and it was time for election. His opponent contrived a story that appeared as though my father had pocketed some money from the county. Although he was cleared of the accusation, he lost the election. It was a bitter political battle with lots of hurt feelings all around. This meant my father would have to find other employment.

From Carson to Winnipeg to Milwaukee

It was 1927, the year Lindbergh made his solo flight across the Atlantic. Because my father and his brothers had been homesteaders, when my dad learned of an opportunity to buy some farmland near Winnipeg, Canada, he was very interested. He had known the man who was the agent for the land, and trusted him without seeing what he was buying. We sold our house, packed all the household goods in a boxcar, and sent it by rail to Winnipeg while we went by car.

Chapter 1

The land deal was a phony. Dad and the others lost everything they had put into it. Mother called her brother, John, in South Milwaukee and told him what had happened. He said to come down to South Milwaukee, and he would find him a job as well as a place for us to live. All our things were never taken out of the freight car, but instead were rerouted to Wisconsin. Uncle John had found a house that we could rent and soon found a carpenter job for my father. The house was large, and had a huge garden plot which my folks put to good use.

It was about time for school to start and I was to enter first grade. As I remember, school was within walking distance, but I had a very poor teacher. We spent most of our time with our heads on our desk sleeping! Needless to say, I didn't learn much and flunked first grade! What a beginning. I'm afraid it had a bad influence on the rest of my life. I've always had difficulty with the use of my time. Whether it is the result of that experience or it is just my weakness, but all my report cards for the next few years had the same observation, "He wastes time."

We lived in that house a little over a year before Dad bought a house with four acres of land more within the city of South Milwaukee. It was almost new and his vision was that each of us would eventually inherit an acre of land. I have several memories about that place. For one thing, we had a large garden. In addition to vegetables, Mother grew many different kinds of flowers. I would go around the neighborhood to sell them. It was great fun pulling my wagon going to all the houses around us. In the process, I made friends with one of the ladies. She would invite me in and on one of the visits she taught me how to read time. But our friendship was short-lived. She had to have an appendectomy and died on the operating table! What a shock that was to me.

We still had the 1921 Dodge that had taken us to Winnipeg and down to South Milwaukee. One day we had driven to Milwaukee to visit Uncle John, who was in the hospital having had one of his fingers amputated because of blood poison. En route home, we were involved in an accident that about killed us all! My father misjudged the speed of the car approaching from our right at the intersection. We were hit broadside so hard the car turned over and almost bounced back to right itself! Adolph went through the windshield, Clarence went through the roof. Both of them only sustained some bruises. Aunt Katie broke her collar bone; I bounced around in the inside of the car. Mother got a few scratches and bruises, but otherwise we were alright. Alta had already gone back to college so was not with us. The car was repaired and we drove it for several more years!

As a family we had become quite close to one of our neighbors. On Sunday afternoon we would often get together to play and sing. My father played the violin, my mother the guitar and the neighbors played the piano and a trumpet. But this was short lived for tragedy soon struck our family.

Tragedy Strikes!

As I mentioned, my father was working as a carpenter building houses. One day he returned home in the mid afternoon sick. He had fainted at work and almost fell off the building! He sat down at the kitchen table and ate a bowl of crackers and milk and I sat on his lap. This was one of his favorite snacks and has been one of mine as well. That was Thursday; by Saturday morning he was dead! He had contracted the 1918 flu which went quickly to his lungs (he was a heavy smoker - two packs a day) which turned into pneumonia. That was August 22, 1929.

Alta was getting ready to return to Fargo to enter her senior year of college; Adolph was going into his senior year of high school; Clarence was entering his sophomore year; and I was going into third grade. Now there was no bread winner and something needed to be done. In talking it over with Uncle John, it was decided that he would pay Mother all Dad had paid for the house and land and he would take over the mortgage. We would rent a house closer in town so that we could take in roomers and boarders. This would give us an income of a sort. Alta was to finish college; Adolph would work half days and go to school the other half and that would give us a bit more income. Clarence and I were too young to do anything, but I do remember I started selling "The Saturday Evening Post" and "Ladies' Home Journal." We lived near a large factory called Bucyrus Erie that built heavy machinery. All was going well until "The Crash" October 29th! Little by little, workers began losing their jobs and we would lose our boarders. Something would have to be done for us to survive.

There are incidents that took place during those months that left a deep impression on my mind. We were at church one Sunday and I could tell my mother was upset. When the service was over she stayed back and waited to talk to the pastor. My mother was a very gentle lady and would go out of her way to avoid a conflict. But she could not put up with what she heard in church that morning. So I heard her say to the pastor, "Rev. Chamberlain, why don't you ever mention the blood of Jesus Christ in you messages?" His response was, "I was not taught that in seminary, but if that's what you want, that's what you'll get."

Another episode on the lighter side happened at the supper table one evening. Adolph earlier somehow had bumped me and I yelled "Ouch!" and he looked at me with a smile and said, "Are you in great pain?" to which I indignantly responded, "Yes!" I determined I was going to get even with him. So I quickly ate my supper and slipped down out my chair under the table. I crawled around until I came to Adolph's feet. I lifted my hand and struck his foot as hard as I could and he yelled "Ouch!" So I stuck my head up from under the table and said to him, "Are you in great pain?!" We all had a good laugh and I felt I had made my point.

Early Years

Back to North Dakota

A filling station near us was put on sale and we thought that perhaps we could operate that and have an income, but people weren't doing much driving, so we could not make ends meet. About that time, Alta's fiancé told us of a farm that was on sale in northern North Dakota. So upon his recommendation, Mother bought the farm and we packed up everything and moved to Nekoma, ND, fifty miles from the Canadian border.

We had a scary experience en route to North Dakota. Adolph was driving and Mother was in the front seat with him and I was squeezed in the back seat with stuff piled up all around me. All of a sudden I saw smoke coming out of the pile and yelled, "Fire!" Adolph stopped the car and we began pulling things out of the back seat. Fortunately there was little damage as we caught it soon and it was under a pile of clothes so it wasn't getting much air. We were all thankful that we didn't lose everything.

Farm Days

Adolph was nineteen years old and totally inexperienced in farming! But Alta's fiancé had just graduated from North Dakota State College in Agricultural Engineering and he said he would help us run the farm. Things did not work out well and he finally left, leaving Adolph with all the responsibility. (Alta broke off the engagement!) The farm was not in very good condition and the equipment was in bad repair and constantly breaking down. In addition, prices for the crops we raised had hit rock bottom. But we were getting by and Adolph was doing better all the time.

I had never lived on a farm, so I had many lessons to learn. It was fun living around animals all the time. When we bought the farm there was a beautiful black and white collie that went with it – we thought. I became very attached to him, but one day the people from whom we had bought the farm came back to take the dog! I heard them talking, so I took the dog and hid him up in the loft of the tool shed. They soon found me and I had to relinquish my dog. (He was a country dog and they took him to Fargo. Within a week he was struck by a car and killed!)

In the winter, it was impossible to drive cars and so we rode to school in a sleigh that looked very much like the prairie schooners you read about in history books. Instead of wheels, were runners. There were benches on either side, and in the middle was a small coal stove bolted to the floor to help keep us warm during the long cold ride. Occasionally, we would put food in the ash bin of the stove to warm it. I would often trade my peanut butter sandwiches for lefse.

There were times when snowstorms would come and either stop us from going to school or would occur while we were at school that would delay our return. There were no telephones (a sleet storm had broken down the lines and they had never been repaired) and of course no cell phones, so parents were left wondering where their children were at times like those. One night we were visiting another farmer, when we got ready to leave a snowstorm had blown in. We had a covered sleigh that would protect us from the elements, but we could not see the heads of the team much of the time. So Adolph dropped the reins and let the horses go. After a few minutes, the horses stopped – right in front of our house! In that part of the country, a rope was strung between the house and the barn so you wouldn't get lost and freeze to death in a snowstorm that could suddenly develop.

There were lots of fun things that can be done on the farm. We always enjoyed playing in the haymow. We could swing on the ropes that were used in bringing the hay into the mow, and it was always a thrill to slide down the stack of hay. We made pets out of many of our animals. My mother talked to all of them. There was a pig and a rooster that would follow her around the barnyard. It was fun watching and listening to them.

Turkeys are a noisy bunch and always seemed to fight with one another. One day I tried to break up the fighting and threw a chunk of dirt at the pair. My aim was not very accurate and instead of hitting the fighters, I hit one of the bystanders in the head! I broke up the fight, but the poor onlooker lay stretched out on the ground. Well, I thought, I'll get some cold water on his head and so I ducked his head in the water tank and drowned him! We had turkey for supper. My mother had a similar experience, but she threw a stick at the fighters, and her aim was better. Again the victim sprawled out on the ground. Mom was disgusted and said to herself, "I'll go in and have a cup of coffee and then come out and dress the bird." When she came out, the turkey was gone, and as she looked around, saw him staggering about like a drunk!

I saw my first mirage while on the farm. As we looked toward the south from the house, there was a clear view for a long way, but that evening, it looked like the ground was a saucer. Instead of the earth being convex, it was concave! You could see nearby towns, and all around were houses with smoke coming out of their chimneys. It was weird! There was another interesting phenomenon. It was only observable at night; a luminous gas would come out of the ground and hover, then disappear. The people around there called them "Jack-o-lanterns." Adolph would often see them at night when he was plowing with the tractor. It was a scary feeling.

From the Farm to Fargo

Finally mother's health failed and we had to leave the farm. If circumstances would have been more favorable, I would have loved to have stayed on the farm. The whole atmosphere was

Chapter 1

wonderful. But God saw fit to move us and put us in an entirely different situation. I moved to Page, ND, where Alta was teaching school, while the farm was being sold and the move was made to Fargo. It was quite an experience to have my own sister as a teacher. I was determined I was not going to be called, "teacher's pet," so I was not the best student in her class! While in Page, I started to play the clarinet, but there wasn't anyone to teach me. However, when I moved to Fargo, where there was a very good music teacher in the junior high I attended. When I got to high school the same teacher continued to work with me both with the clarinet as well as voice. So I was in the band, orchestra, men's glee club, mixed choir, male quartet, mixed quartet, and even vocal solo work. He was really an inspiration to me.

We moved during my ninth grade. The music teacher in the second junior high school was also a great help. He sang with a group called T*he Amphiun Male Choir.* He brought my good friend, Charlie Dills, and I into that choir. We were both fifteen

Early Years

and the oldest member was seventy-five. That year the choir was invited to sing with John Charles Thomas, a famous opera singer, at the Indiana Theater in Indianapolis, IN. While on the tour, we sang at Notre Dame in South Bend, IN, and in Chicago. It was a unique experience for a couple of teenagers.

Spiritually our whole family had drifted away from the Lord. Mother had always been the spiritual leader of the family, but when she became critically ill with diabetes, we all stopped going to church. One of the reasons was we could not find a church that preached the gospel. One day mother found a wonderful gospel broadcast called *The Old Fashioned Revival Hour*. As mother continued asking me to listen to the program with her, little by little I became interested in more than the good music that was part of the hour long program. Then one day mother discovered a local daily fifteen minute gospel broadcast, and we started listening to that as well. The speaker's church was just two blocks from where we lived, so we began attending their services. It was a German Evangelical Church. The pastor's name was Rev. Reuben Strutz. His messages were practical and warm, but once in awhile he would become so carried away that he would start preaching in German and of course, I lost him!

By this time, mother's health had improved, and we bought a boarding and rooming house. There are several aspects about that house that were outstanding to me, especially in the winter.

I could put on my ice skates in the kitchen, slide down the hill in back of our house right on to a lighted, four blocks long skating rink with a nice warming house.

One year, I believe it was 1939, Clarence had moved back in with us and brought his shortwave "rig" with him. It was a particularly hard winter and much of the telephone and telegraph wires were down. Clarence's "ham radio" became the center of communication for quite sometime, which gave him a lot of publicity, and later an invitation to join the US Signal Corp. (Because he was partially blind, he joined as a civilian. This launched him on a career that he would follow the rest of his life.) That was the same year I went over to visit Bob Steidl one night. We were playing games and were not paying any attention to what the weather was doing, when my mother called and said, "Have you looked outside?" A blizzard had blown in and it was impossible to walk home. So I spent the night with the Steidls. Bob and I had been friends since eighth grade and the relationship continues to this day.

College and New Life in Christ!

From the time I was a little boy, it was my ambition to become a medical missionary to China, though I had never met a missionary. No doubt it was the result of my mother's prayers. In high school I took all the math, science, and language courses that would prepare me to enter a pre-med course in college. I graduated from high school in May, 1940, and in the fall, I enrolled in North Dakota State College in their pre-med school. I had enough money to get through the first year, but that was all! I would have to drop out and go to work in order to return to college.

During the Christmas break in 1940, the Fargo Rescue Mission was holding a revival service in connection with the dedication of their new building. On the last night of the series, our church dismissed so we could all attend the mission's service. Bob Steidl and I walked over together. At the close of the service an invitation to accept Jesus Christ as Savior was given and I knew I needed to do that, so I went forward and was led to the Lord by Mr. Halverson, a Presbyterian elder. We were members of a German Evangelical church; this was a Free Methodist mission; and the evangelist was from the Assemblies of God. I tell people, that's why I'm a Baptist minister today!! My mother had been in the service that night and saw me walk down to the front. Her heart was overjoyed! When we got home, she told me the prayer she had made before I was born and that this was what she was waiting for before telling me. I could see then why I had the desire to be a medical missionary to China.

Chapter 1

A Major Change!

Several of us college students were facing the same problem of having to drop out of school in order to earn enough to go back. There was an ad in the paper telling of opportunities for jobs in the new defense factories that were opening up around the country. Four of us went to the City Hall and took an examination that would determine what kind of plant we would be qualified in which to work. While waiting for an answer from the defense plants, I was worked in a bakery for twenty-five cents an hour. I needed to do better than that if I intended to go back to college. I finally landed a job with a local taxicab company. I was elated, and told my Pastor Strutz. His response? "Over my dead body!" He went to the phone and in a few minutes came back and said, "You can start work tomorrow at a Christian insurance company for fifty cents an hour." Twice the minimum wage!

No one that had taken the examination at City Hall had heard anything, when in the middle of July, 1941, I received a letter from Lockheed Aircraft factory in Burbank, CA, stating I had a job with them starting August 4, at ninety-five cents an hour as a radio electrician! (I was the first one to get a response!) As my mother, our pastor, and I prayed about it, it was felt this was of the Lord and that I should take the offer. I was leaving home for the first time in my life at nineteen years of age, and going to a place where I would be a complete stranger. It was going to be a big change! I had ten days to get to Burbank so I decided to stop by Walla Walla, WA, to visit my sister and her family. I was traveling by bus, but it didn't go through Walla Walla so I made arrangements to get off at the junction of two highways near Walla Walla. There was a filling station near that junction, but the driver let me off on the highway and I had to walk in the dark to the filling station. It was midnight! Shortly after I reached the station, Alta and Walter arrived. Was I ever glad to see them!

Early Years

I stayed three days before catching the bus for Burbank. The weather was getting hotter and hotter the further south we went until we arrived in Redding, CA, where the thermometer told us it was 106! There was no air-conditioning on the busses – just the air that came in the windows and that was hot. (In those days there was an expression about air-conditioning. It was 4/40, which meant four windows open at forty miles an hour!) It was Saturday afternoon, August 2, when I arrived in Burbank. The bus didn't let me off at a station, but just a local stop. The driver gave me my suitcase, and I stood there bewildered. I remember saying aloud, "OK, Lord, where do I go now?"

God's supply

Tujunga Boulevard "T's" into Main Street, so I picked up my suitcase and started walking up Tujunga Blvd. In about two blocks, there was a sign in the front yard of a house saying they accepted roomers and boarders. I went in and found what I liked. It was a garage that had been converted into a sort of dorm with four of us as roommates. The landlady said, "After you get settled, come on in for supper." As soon as we were seated, she announced that they were Christians and went to church on Sunday. If any of us wanted to go with them, they would be welcome! (Blessings number 1 and 2!) The next morning after breakfast, we went to church and Sunday school. What a wonderful church! The Pastor as well as the youth leader were men of God. We were fed the Word in the morning and evening services. After the evening service, the youth fellowship met and discussed what the pastor had preached in the evening service. What a way to grow in the Lord.

One of the youth activities was to go down to what was called "Skid Row" (the red light district of LA) where we had the opportunity to give our testimonies, take part in street services, hand out tracts, and lead singing. I read my Bible, and the Word became more meaningful. Another weekend, we went as a group to the mountains to what was called Forest Hills Bible Camp. There were several outstanding speakers from around the country. I had never been to anything like that in my life. One of the speakers was Dick Halverson, a converted dance band leader, who later became chaplain of the US Senate. He was the nephew of the man who had led me to the Lord in Fargo! (Several years later when I was Pacific Broadcasting Association's Rep, Hatori Sensei and I visited him in Washington, DC.)

Decision and Consequences

I began to learn more about the Gospel, and asked a lot of questions. I saw in the Scriptures for the first time, when people were saved, it was followed by water baptism. This had not been my experience, so I went to the pastor and asked him about it. As a Lutheran, I had been sprinkled as a babe. So I asked the pastor if I could be baptized by immersion, and he said, "Yes." I'll never forget that experience. It was an immense blessing.

I was so thrilled about what I had learned, and that I had been immersed. I wrote in great detail to my mother, who I thought would be just as thrilled as I was. But, alas, that was not the case. She shared the letter with Pastor Strutz, who wrote me a very stinging letter saying I had forsaken all the teaching that my mother had given me and that I had not consulted her before doing this. I was stunned! The two people who I had such confidence in and loved so dearly had condemned me for what I had done! The upshot of it all was, my mother sold the rooming and boarding house in Fargo, and came to live with me. That was November, 1941. She didn't want me to be led astray by some strange doctrine. So I rented a house and bought a car. She went with me to church every Sunday and enjoyed it. It never became a problem, but she never submitted to baptism by immersion.

It seemed that everyone in Burbank worked at Lockheed "Roses are red; violets are blue, I work at Lockheed and so do you!" I

Early Years

enjoyed my work and organized a noon lunch Bible study under the wing of a P38! We never had more then five or six, but it was a new experience that would shape my life for what the Lord had before me.

I tried to show Mom around the LA area and one Sunday afternoon we were in Pasadena and had the radio on, when suddenly the program was interrupted and the announcement that Pearl Harbor had been attacked by the Japanese and America had declared war on Japan and Germany! That was stunning. Mom turned to me and said, "I suppose that means you'll have to go to war!" I said, "That depends how long it lasts. I'm working in a defense plant and I'm also your sole support."

I continued to work at Lockheed and attend First Baptist Church until one day a poster at work announced a naval program that was seeking volunteers in electronics. I shared the information with Mom and said, "It looked like men at Lockheed were being drafted, and I am sure that I will eventually be called." So with Mom's consent, I took the entrance exam to see if I qualified and I did. I was to launch into a new phase of my life that would shape me for the work I would eventually be doing on the mission field.

Military Years & Continued Growth in Christ

On October 1, 1942 the bus taking us from LA to Boot Camp in San Diego pulled into the naval base to the chorus of sailors standing around the gate singing "You'll be sorry! You'll be sorry!" But that night as I lay in my bunk praying, I had sweet peace knowing I was in the very spot I was supposed to be in the will of God. Boot Camp usually is several months in duration, but in war time, everything is rushed and it was just a month. During that time we had a battery of shots. We were lined up at the door of "sickbay" (navy clinic) and as we walked through the door we were given shots in both arms! Then we were marched out on the drill field and put through all kinds of calisthenics. We thought they were trying to kill us before we even got started in the service, but actually they were helping us. Without the exercises we would have been worse. There were many that checked into sickbay that night, but I ended up just having some very stiff arms. The next day I had to go to the main office with some questions. They had me wait outside on the veranda. All of a sudden I felt rather dizzy and sat down on one of the benches thinking it was from the shots, but as I looked up, I saw the light fixtures hanging from the ceiling swinging back and forth! I was experiencing my first earthquake!

One drill I will never forget was to teach us how to jump off a ship in case of an emergency. We were fully clothed and were to jump off a twenty foot tower into the pool, take off our trousers while treading water, tie a knot in the bottom of each pant leg, swing the pants over our heads to fill the legs with air, then use them to keep us afloat. There was only one way off the tower – jump! The longer I waited, the higher the tower seemed to get until finally I leaped!

Texas A&M

When we finished boot camp, we were sent to Texas A&M, College Station, TX. There were four hundred in our company. We were to embark on a crash program in electrical engineering. Our accommodations were wonderful. We lived in the school dorms with two per room and were fed scrumptiously! We were in classes eight hours a day and the evenings were for study. Every morning before breakfast at 5 a.m. we had "Happy Hour"

Early Years

(calisthenics) rain or shine! I wish now I had taken advantage of those weekends to travel around a bit, but instead I used most of the time studying for the next week's assignments.

The course in engineering was equivalent to two and a half year's credit should we continue with those studies after the war. However, we did it in three months! To say the least, it was highly concentrated. There were four hundred in our company when we arrived; there were just over one hundred when we graduated! Every week there were many who were shipped out as they couldn't keep up with the pace. I had a roommate who claimed to be a Christian, but he was not a good influence in my walk with the Lord. When I was saved I stopped going to dances and the movies, but under the influence of my roommate, I started going to both; my whole spiritual life seemed to come to a standstill. I read my Bible, but not much praying.

Corpus Christi or San Francisco?

Just before we graduated, we were given a choice as to what our next training would be. If we wanted to study shipboard electronics, we would go to Treasure Island, San Francisco, CA. If we wanted to study airborne electronics, we would be assigned to Corpus Christi, TX. I really didn't know which one to choose, so I turned my paper in blank and trusted the Lord to send me where He wanted. I ended up in Corpus. It was a major point in my life. How different my life would have been had I chosen Treasure Island!

I was given a two weeks furlough between assignments, so I decided to visit Alta and her family in Walla Walla, WA, as that's where my mother was at the time. (Incidentally, the Navy sent Mom monthly support the whole time I was in the service.) We had a wonderful time together. I hitchhiked on military planes going and returning. My first stop was Oklahoma City. I had a layover of two hours before my next flight, so I went to the USO. Of course it was filled with GIs, but I thought I saw a familiar face and walked over to where he was, and sure enough, it was Bob Steidl! We had a wonderful two hours together.

I'll never forget my arrival in Corpus. It was March 3, 1943. A "Norther" was blowing in and it was raining! I was wearing my "blues" and had my "P coat" on and I was still cold! I walked around on the "T Heads" for a while before catching the bus to Ward Island, the naval base where I was to be stationed. The accommodations were nothing like what we had at Texas A & M. We were in barracks with bunk beds and a locker at the head of each bunk where we stored all we possessed.

Again every morning was "Happy Hour," then to breakfast. At 8 we lined up in front of the barracks and marched into the restricted area where the school was. There were twelve large barracks: six were for class rooms where theory was taught and six were for the laboratories where the practical (hands on experience) was taught. The course was six months in which you would spend a month in each section. So there was a lecture building and lab building for each section where different pieces of equipment were studied.

Early Years

A Spiritual Battle

These were days of learning, not just in electronics, but also in my spiritual life. As I said earlier, my walk with the Lord was in shambles! I had a "form of Godliness," but there was no power in my life. I tried to organize a Bible study on the base, but not many turned out. I was going to dances at the USO, and "choosing" my movies. I even starting smoking! One Saturday afternoon one of my fellow students who had been my foreman at Lockheed came by as I was washing clothes and smoking my pipe. He looked at me for a moment and said, "Bernie, you've slipped a long ways since you joined the Navy!" A Christian buddy from another barracks came by to see me and I thought his lower jaw would fall off as he saw me smoking. But none of these fazed me.

A couple of weeks later I went to a USO dance. The next day I was scheduled to sing at the USO chapel service. When I finished singing, I started walking back to the First Baptist Church and I really felt down. I always carried my New Testament with me and I took it out of my pocket and it fell open to II Corinthians 6. Verse 3 seemed to be in bold print! "Giving no offence in anything, that the ministry be not blamed!" My whole life spread out before me and I saw that the things I was doing which were an offense to the Gospel. I certainly was not living a consistent Christian life. When I arrived at the church, I saw Howard Butt, with whom I had a lot of contact and asked him if he would go into one of the Sunday school rooms and pray with me. I told him how the Lord had just dealt with me, and the Scripture verse He had shown me. We had a word of prayer together and I rededicated my life to the Lord. What had happened to me was real, and I intended, by God's grace, to live a life for Christ from then on. The Wednesday night Bible study started to grow and fellows were being saved. The chaplain let us use the chapel, and the meetings were announced over the PA system that went into all the barracks, even the chiefs' and officers'.

Chapter 1

Outside activities

Ted Johnson, Bill Kredit, Don Hattrum and I formed what we called "The Ward Island Quartet." We received invitations to sing in several churches. It was a wonderful opportunity to sing

as well as give our testimonies. Life-long friendships were formed in those days, in fact even now, one of Bill and Evelyn Kredit's daughters, Barb and her husband, George Anderson, are close friends of our daughter and her husband.

Gas and tires were rationed and few people had cars in those days, but those that did would pick up sailors going to and from the two bases (Main Base which was for flight training, and Ward Island, which was the electronics school.) The buses going to town started at Main base. By the time they came to Ward Island, they were full so we would hitch a ride as best we could. My hitchhiking verse was Romans 3:12, "They are all gone out of the way, they are together become unprofitable; there is none that doeth good, no, not one!"

Returning to the base at night was another problem. If you didn't go to the bus depot, but tried to board at one of the stops, you ran the risk of not being able to get on because of the crowd! There were straps to hang on to if you were standing, but there was little need for them because you were supported by the others standing around you! I remember at times falling asleep and catching myself when my knees buckled! I felt sorry for the short fellows; they would be almost smothered. I often wondered how the buses stood up because they were always overloaded.

New Assignment

Mom, who had come down to Corpus to be with me while I was in school, figured I'd be going to sea after graduation, so she de-

cided to go back to Chicago to live with her sister-in-law. I was glad she would be near family. However, when it came time to graduate, Ted Johnson, Bill Kredit and I were among those who were asked to stay on as instructors. This enabled us to continue our quartet (we had to find another second tenor) and I could keep leading the weekly Bible study which was then averaging over 50 in attendance.

The Wednesday Bible study was really an evangelistic outreach where we would try to bring unsaved to the meetings. But a group became interested in having a more concentrated Bible study and meet on Saturday afternoons. There was an old building on the base that wasn't being used for anything and we were given permission to meet there. I contacted Dawson Trotman, founder of The Navigators, a Christian servicemen's organization. They had a Bible study and Scripture memory program which was very helpful to us.

An older fellow from the youth group at First Baptist took me aside one evening and started talking about a deeper life in Christ. Of course I was interested in that. I was only a couple of years old in the faith and had much to learn. I soon discovered what he had in mind was to teach me to speak in tongues. That was something I didn't know anything about. On one occasion, I had an experience with him that frightened me. In trying to get me to speak in tongues, I suddenly felt paralyzed and could not speak at all! I wrote to Dawson Trotman and told him what I had experienced and asked if he could help me. He wrote me a long letter and sent me three wonderful books and recommended a study Bible – a Thompson Chain Reference. My eyes were opened and I began to study my Bible to know what I believed and why. I thank God for the Navigators, especially the Bible memory program. The next few years were like seminary training for me. My life was being shaped for the ministry I was to enter when I got out of the Navy.

As an instructor, life was very interesting. I had a reputation that spread through the base that no one was allowed to curse in my classes. Sometimes we were given new pieces of equipment that had little information on them, so we would have to write an instruction manual in order to teach. (That's where I learned to type.) At the end of each session, the students were given what was called a "gripe sheet" which they were to fill out to help us know how we could improve what we were doing. One time, of the 33 students I had, 31 had the same gripe – "He talks too fast." I'm afraid I still have that problem!

New Developments

The Saturday afternoon Bible study was a much smaller group. There were about twelve of us. One Saturday someone mentioned having a "street service" in downtown Corpus. We all agreed to meet at the bus depot and march down Main Street to the city park and hold our evangelistic meeting on the street in front of the park. The "Shore Patrol" (Navy Police) drove by a couple of times and stopped. We were told we couldn't have a meeting like that and our Liberty Cards were taken from us. We were to report to the base commander on Monday. He was very understanding, but said we would have to get a church to sponsor us. We knew of a good church that we thought would sponsor us, Calvary Baptist, and the pastor, Rev. Theo Binford, was delighted and said he would recommend the young people from the church to take part with us.

Is She The One?

With the church sponsorship we were free to continue the street meetings together with the young people of Calvary Baptist. On one of the first meetings there was a young lady from the church who gave her testimony. She really caught my attention. There were other young ladies there too, but there was something special about this one! She carried the biggest Bible I had ever seen and when she finished reading from it, she would lay it on her shoulder and give her testimony. Then she would read some more verses and make comment. I nudged the sailor next to me and said, "I'm going to marry that girl!" I don't remember talking with her that evening, but a few weeks later at another church we met and I introduced myself.

There were other occasions where the fellows from Ward Island would seek ways in which to give our testimonies at churches. There were three of us together one Sunday after noon: Dan Sickler, Wayne Gute, and me. Dan had an apartment in town and we were meeting at his place. After we had prayed for awhile, Dan said he had read of a new church that was celebrating its first anniversary that Sunday afternoon. It was just a couple blocks from where we were, so we decided to walk over and see if we would be able to give our testimonies. When the minister had finished his remarks he asked if there were any who would like to give a testimony. Dan got up and told how he had come to know the Lord. Then Wayne gave his testimony and I gave mine last. But the surprise of the afternoon was to see the young lady I had seen at the street meeting also in attendance. I could hardly wait till the meeting was over to meet her. We talked a long time after the service. I was thrilled to meet a young lady who really loved the Lord and wanted to follow Him.

The next week I received a call from Jeanette asking me to speak the following Sunday night to the young people of the little Methodist church, which I did. Her next younger sister was with her and was saved. I could hardly wait to walk them home. After prayer, I returned to the base.

When I heard that on September 24th Jeanette had gone forward to dedicate her life to the Lord for foreign missions, it was a confirmation that she was the Lord's choice for me. On November 4, Jeanette and I were sitting on the front porch where she and Grandma Miller lived. I suggested we pray about working together. On November the 11th I asked her to marry me and on the 12th we were engaged. Everyone thought we should get married and so did we. Many warned Jeanette that if she married me, there would never be a dull moment. (And she says, "There never has been!") Since it was the custom in those days, Jeanette thought it would be good if I asked her father if I could have his daughter in marriage which I did. Then the time seemed to pass too slowly, but we had many friends with whom to visit and church services to attend until April 6, our wedding day.

WEDDING BELLS - Jeanette

On April 6, 1945, we were married in Calvary Baptist Church with Rev. Theo Binford officiating. I asked my daddy to give me

away and he was quite excited to do so; it was also his birthday. I have often wondered with my relationship to my daddy as it was, why I would ask him to give me away, but I have never been sorry. Our attendants were Kris and Opal Solberg, Ted Johnson, and Doris Fanchier. My brother, Earl Miller and Maurice Hammond were ushers. We were honored to have Howard Butt, Jr. as our soloist (the son of the owner of the famous HEB stores of Texas.) His accompanist was Mrs. Flora Fae Ryerson.

In his officiating sermon, Pastor Binford mentioned that our plans were to be missionaries. As a testimony we asked Howard to sing "Footsteps of Jesus," of which the words of the last verse are:

> Sweetly Lord we have heard Thee calling,
> Come follow me...
> Though they lead o're the cold dark mountain

> Feeding His sheep...
> Then on high, our journey done
> We will rest where the steps of Jesus
> End at His throne.

After the song, Pastor Binford said there wasn't a dry eye in the church; it was like an evangelistic meeting. When the ceremony was finished, Bernie and I drove away in Howard's car. We parked under a street lamp and dedicated our lives to the service of our Lord and Savior.

Chapter Two
Preparations for Missionary Service

College Days - Bernie

It was only reasonable, if we wanted to be missionaries, we would need some training. While Jeanette was still at the naval base and I in the Navy, we needed to make a choice as to which

school we would attend. We were already accepted at Wheaton College, in Wheaton, IL. Then one day we heard Dr. Bob Jones, Jr. was to speak in San Antonio, we decided to attend the meet-

Preparation

ing. After hearing him and praying about the decision, we felt it was the Lord's leading for us to enter Bob Jones College (BJC), located in Cleveland, TN. Bernie was discharged Dec. 17, 1945, and school would be starting Jan. 26, 1946. It was a new venture, but how would we ever make it? The GI Bill covered my tuition, and books, but only $95 a month on which to live! After settling down on the train, Jeanette began singing, "All the way my Savior leads me, what have I to ask besides?" How we needed the words of that song! We enjoyed our first semester of college.

We were invited to work with The Church of the Open Door in Greenville, Miss., for the summer months which changed our lives in many ways. Flora Fae Ryerson's father, Bro. H. O. Langston, was the pastor of the church and she and her husband Jim became our dearest friends. Actually we had met Jim and Flora Fae while we were still in the service. Jim was a flight instructor at the naval air base and Flora Fae had played the piano at our wedding. Bro. and Mrs. Langston became "Mom and Dad" to us.

The Birth of Karen Bernette – Jeanette

We went back to BJC in the fall. We had lived in a very small trailer the last semester, but when we came back the trailer was no longer available so we rented a room in a private home near the college. During the year, I knew I was expecting and decided to go back to Greenville, MS, with the Langstons six weeks before the school year ended. I stayed in school through the first semester, but dropped out the second and continued schooling by correspondence from the University of Texas. Bernie stayed on in the room we had rented and counted the days until we could be back together again. Karen's arrival date was about the same as the last day of school. So without telling me, Bernie moved all his exams up and was able to leave school early. As the train was pulling into Greenville, Bernie thought he had better call

Bro. Langston and ask what the best way to tell me that he was there. Bro. Langston figured out a scheme and brought me to the depot to meet Bernie. I was totally surprised and glad to see him. Donna Bernette was born the next day! The date was May 31, 1947.

The day after Donna was born, Bernie came to the hospital to find me crying. I said, "I just can't call her Donna; she's Karen." The reason for the confusion was that shortly before our Karen

was born, Bernie's brother, Adolph, and his wife had adopted a little girl and called her Karen Jeanne. We thought that it would never do to have two Karen Holritzes. When Bernie heard my plea, he quickly ran to the hospital office. Sure enough, the birth certificate was still there and they scratched through the name "Donna" and replaced it with, "Karen." Bernie's mom came down from Chicago to see her new granddaughter and to help out in anyway she could. She stayed on after we left for school and got a job taking care of the mother of a lady who lived on a large plantation just outside of Greenville.

When we finished the last semester in Cleveland, the school announced that they had sold the campus and were moving to

Preparation

Greenville, SC. That meant that we would have to find a place to live when we returned for the fall semester. The Ryersons learned of the sale of surplus army trailers which could be fixed up and used for housing. We were both able to buy one and they

were parked in the Langston's backyard where we completely rebuilt them. So we spent the summer working for the church and rebuilding our trailers. But how were we going to get our trailer to SC in as much as we did not have a car?! On the Sunday night before we were to leave for SC, our trailers were pulled to the church so that everybody could see them. During the service, Bro. Langston announced that we needed to get our trailer to South Carolina, but didn't have a car to pull it. The church took up an offering to cover the cost of a truck that would not only pull our trailer, but also the extra things that were too heavy to put in the trailers. Another miracle!

Back at school, we quickly settled in a trailer camp, and were joined by many other GIs who had bought trailers as well. Our trailer park was right across the street from what is now called Bob Jones University. There we developed a camaraderie with Jim & Eileen Bell, Thornton & Millie Weymouth, and Homer & Mary Leventry, in addition to the Ryersons. We had to make things stretch in order to live on $95 per month. We were thankful that some of the students had cars so we would get together and shop at a huge grocery store that sold their merchandise at a discount. Ginny Sue Bell and our Karen were only three days apart in age and loved playing together. Their favorite game was, "The Bible Class" in which one would stand on a chair and "direct" the singing while the other sat on a chair and did the singing!

While building our small trailer, the only place we could find for Karen's bed was right across the foot of ours. It was like an ordinary crib with spindles to keep her from falling out as well a section to store her toys. As she got a little older, she found she could climb over the spindles and jump out of her bed sometimes landing on our stomachs. Then she would crawl to find her daddy's shoes, almost too big for her to carry, stick them in his face and say, "It's time to get up, Daddy."

One morning she and I decided to go to the bath/commode house early. When it was time to leave the bathhouse, Karen did not want to go. So I tried to pull her by her hand, finally I picked her up to hasten the trip. But she was so angry that she held her breath until she passed out in my arms and scared me to death! She never held her breath again as it frightened her as well.

Our Call to Japan – Bernie and Jeanette

From the time Bernie was a boy, he had always planned to be a missionary to China. It was also the conviction of Jeanette's heart as well. During the last semester before Bernie was to graduate, Dr. Norman Grubb of World Evangelistic Crusade spoke to the Saturday Mission Prayer Band. He had just completed a global survey trip to see what mission opportunities there were available after WWII. Among other things he told of the unique opportunity for radio evangelism in Japan. Jeanette had not attended the meeting as she was taking care of Karen back in the trailer. When Bernie came home, he reviewed with Jeanette all he had heard and suggested we consider the possibility of going to Japan instead of China.

Preparation

Jeanette's response was, "If that's where you think we should go, let's go!" What a tremendous decision, and with such ease! Shortly after that, the doors of China were closed to missionaries- a wonderful confirmation! This was the spring of 1948.

We decided to spend the summer with the family of Bernie's best friend from childhood, Mr. & Mrs. M. T. Steidl, Mom & Dad to Bernie. While we were there something tragic almost happened. Bernie awoke one morning with a whooping kind of cough, but could not get his breath. Soon the entire Steidl family was by his side with Dick, a pre-med student forcing him to the floor to give him CPR while Mom Steidl called Emergency shouting, "He's gone! He's gone!" Fortunately Bernie was soon able to breath normally again and learned how to do so with following attacks. A doctor was called who said that Bernie had a nervous breakdown, and in any case would never be able to go to Japan as a missionary!

A few days later, our little Karen started coughing in the same way as Bernie, and Jeanette wondered if both of them might have whooping cough. A doctor confirmed what Jeanette had supposed. (When we returned to BJU in the fall, we found that two members of the radio quartet Bernie sang in also had whooping cough during the summer.) With Bernie and Karen healed – a miracle – we were still on our way to Japan.

Just before Bernie was to graduate, we received a phone call from Mississippi telling us that Bernie's mother had been taken in an ambulance unconscious to the ER in Greenville and that we should come. A fellow student loaned us his car to drive to Mississippi. Mother had died before we arrived! Gangrene had set in in both legs from her diabetes. We took her body to South Milwaukee to be buried next to my father, then hurried back to South Carolina in time for Bernie to take his final exams. Mother had written a letter and mailed a birthday package to Karen the day before she died. They were both waiting for us when we got back to South Carolina!

Bernie graduated in May, 1949. Karen was very excited on the day of graduation. Several packages that had come, but in her

Preparation

mind he was not opening them fast enough. So she tried to get his attention and said, "Open your 'gradumuashum!'" But Bernie didn't pay any attention. So she said, "Open your birthday!" But when he still didn't move, she finally shouted, "Open your picnic, Daddy!"

Obstacles!

We spent our last few months before leaving for Japan in Greenville, Miss. with our dear friends of the Church of the Open Door. We had a Chevy Carry All (made possible by the inheritance from Bernie's mother). We pulled our trailer, and parked it behind the home of the E. B. Glazes, who were like grandma and grandpa to us.

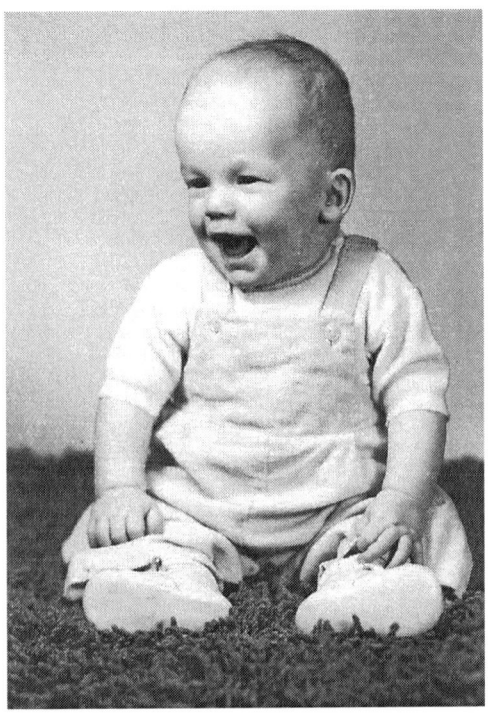

While there, our second child, Paul Jonathan, was born, August 4, 1949. The next morning Jeanette had the strangest feeling like

Chapter 2

something weird was happening to her. She grabbed her New Testament and started crying out to the Lord. The lady in the bed next to her asked, "Did you have a spinal?" To which Jeanette replied, "Yes." Then she said, "That's why you have a problem. I have a friend who had a spinal and she went crazy!"

Jeanette had a similar thought put in her mind before we left Bob Jones by a friend who said she had a dream that Jeanette had gone crazy. Her condition did not improve. Her physician suggested she go to Memphis, TN, to seek a psychiatrist's opinion. He said, "Are you still planning to go to Japan? With the change in climate, language, and customs, you'll never make it more than a year." Bernie asked her what she wanted to do, and she said, "I want to go ahead." During the next year before we went to Japan, it wasn't easy for Jeanette, but she managed to keep her equilibrium. This was also true in Japan, but the Lord gave us 18 years of fruitful ministry.

Another obstacle came in the form of a telephone call. We were waiting for the sailing date to be established when we received a call from Brother Langston. They had been involved in a near fatal accident and were both seriously injured. They asked if we would postpone our going to Japan and take the pastorate of the Church of the Open Door for a year. As we prayed about it, we felt that the momentum was to go, and if we stopped then, we might never get to the field. It was a very hard decision to make, but we knew it was God's answer.

We left Greenville MS pulling our trailer and stopping for meetings along the way seeking to raise our passage money as we traveled to Corpus Christi. The most we ever received in offerings was $10 to $25 hardly enough to get us to the next place. It was the night before the deadline our mission had set to have a thousand dollars on hand and we were far from that goal. Miraculously through the contact of a friend in SC, a meeting in Harlingen, TX, near the Mexican border, opened up. We got the

Preparation

usual offering. When all the lights were turned off and Bernie was putting his equipment in the car, a man startled him out of the dark and asked what we needed to get to Japan. He answered, "A thousand dollars," and with tears in his eyes he wrote a check for the thousand dollars. Praise the Lord, we were on our way to Japan. (We tried to contact him when we returned on furlough to thank him, but he showed no interest. The Lord had him there for one particular need and that was it!)

Chapter Three
Ministry in Japan 1950 ~ 1968

First Term: 1950 ~ 1955

Preparation for and sailing to Japan

It was 1950 and we were anxious to get underway, but imagine shopping with a grocery list for five years, plus furniture, clothing for two growing children as well as other needed items. In

spite of our preparations, we would still have to shop for other groceries from Overseas Stores, quite a distance from our home and time consuming. We couldn't shop on the Japanese market because it was unable even to sustain the nationals!

Ministry in Japan

We were originally scheduled to sail from Seattle on March 17, but due to problems on the ship, we were rescheduled to sail from Portland, OR, on March, 28. Because of the change, we were able to spend some time with "Bernie's sister and her family in Vancouver. British Columbia. This delay in sailing also made our military permits to enter Japan invalid. So we left Seattle on March 27th not knowing if we would be sailing the next day.

We wired Washington to see what could be done to get another permit. Sailing was again delayed another two days. Miraculously the new permit arrived two hours before we had to board the ship! Sometime after midnight, we stood on the deck and waved goodbye to America as the SS Java Mail set its course toward Japan.

Since we were on the freighter on Easter Sunday, the captain asked Bernie to bring a message. Two people raised their hands for salvation. After twelve days and no sea sickness, we arrived in Yokohama. The only one of our family who didn't enjoy the trip was our eight month old son, Paul. When we passed through fog, the ship's horn would blow and Paul would cry.

Chapter 3

Our arrival and first house

If we expected Japanese or a group of missionaries standing on the dock to welcome us, we must have been greatly disappointed for there was no one! We looked the wharf over and found our Chevy Suburban Carryall (which had come on another ship) standing in a holding area. Then Bernie scouted around the dock and discovered an older gentleman asleep in his car. It was our mission's field chairman, who had come to welcome us. He apologized and said because our ship was delayed he had fallen asleep. Since we had our car, we were able to drive ourselves to the mission headquarters in Tokyo. Jeanette was impressed with the crowds as well as the bombed out buildings, but Bernie had his hands full trying to get used to driving on the left side of the road!

The next day we moved into our Japanese house and realized how much we had cut our ties with the American style of living. We had to pump all our water and boil that which was used for drinking. At the far end of the hall was our "in door - out door" toilet, with no seat, which the "honey bucket" man emptied once a month! Because of the close proximity of the houses, frequently at night we would hear noises downstairs as if someone was trying to break in. Can you imagine Bernie at two a.m. trying to ward off a burglar by throwing a shoe down the stairs only to find it was noises from next door? Later we were told it would be better to stay in bed rather than confronting a burglar!

When we looked out the windows of our house, we could see rice paddies for the first time. There were lots of children running around and they were very interested to see what the "gaijin" (foreigners) had in their house and what they were doing. For the most part, we did not sense any resentment toward us as Americans. On the contrary, they were very friendly. This was due in great measure to the action of General Macarthur, who came in, not as a mighty conqueror, but as one who wanted to help Japan get reestablished. We are so thankful that our mission chooses to have their missionaries live among the people rather than in compounds. This makes it easier to get acquainted with their mode of living, become friends, and eventually lead them to the Lord. One aspect of life in Japan which we were not aware of until one morning when we were handed some capsules and told this was the beginning of our regular scheduled dose of medicine for parasites! I'll not tell you the reaction to the medication or even the name of the parasites less you get the same nauseous feeling we had!

Having arrived in 1950, we were in several unusual situations. The missionary children had to have a place to go to school. Immediately, Bernie found himself on the school board of the Christian Academy in Japan (CAJ) and often drove the bus which would occupy most of the day. In addition, we were supposed to study Japanese eight hours a day, but the Japanese language is considered the most difficult in the world. For example, if you were speaking to a doctor or a preacher, you would use a more polite language, but if you were speaking to a student, or a

Chapter 3

clerk or even a dog you would us a less formal language (Even newspaper language was different.) In a husband/wife relationship, the husband is called "lord" and she is beneath his dignity.

We have already introduced you to CAJ, a school for missionary children started by evangelical missionaries. The school bought

the land and building of what had been the dairy farm of the Emperor with plenty of room for expansion. The luxurious cow barns were converted into classrooms. The need for finances, but especially for teachers, was unusually desperate. So far, those who were teaching came for the purpose of evangelizing Japanese – not teaching missionary children. We tried to get teachers who were called of God for this task, but the sending churches were often not sympathetic. On one occasion, when a lady was coming to Japan to teach missionary children, her home church cut off her support.

The radio ministry - Bernie

Before leaving for Japan, we had an interview with Dr. David Johnson, General Director of The Evangelical Alliance Mission (TEAM) (at that time it was known as The Scandinavian Alliance Mission). He had reviewed our application and noticed our experience in radio. Dr. Johnson mentioned the vision of six missions in Japan, of which TEAM was one, who were seeking permits for Christian radio stations, as Japan had announced it would have commercial radio for the first time in its history. He suggested that we consider radio evangelism as a ministry. Two weeks after arriving in Japan, at TEAM's spring field conference, I was asked to be one of the members of the radio commission that was negotiating with the Japanese government for permits.

After months of tedious deliberation, the government's reply was, "We will not grant a permit to any one religion, but if the Protestants, Catholics, Shintoists and Buddhists will combine to form one organization, we will grant a permit." Such, of course, was untenable. The result was, two missions, TEAM and FEGC, asked three men from each mission to form an organization to produce radio programs and buy time on the newly organized commercial stations. That was the beginning of what was then known as Pacific Orient Broadcasting Company (POBC).

Satan was never far away and he did everything he could to stop us. One of the first places was getting organized ourselves: who was to do what? We found ourselves divided, not just by missions, but by philosophy. Three of us thought we should wait until we had everything working perfectly, and three of us felt we should take advantage of what we had, start producing programs, and buying time. It all came to a head one day as the six of us met at our home. It was a power struggle! But instead of blowing up, God melted our hearts together, and we became one. Interestingly enough, that day one of the missions that had been part of the radio commission voted to give POBC the money they had raised for the proposed radio stations. It was our first gift and the only money we had! What a miracle! Now we were ready to work. Each was assigned an area of responsibility – mine was follow-up.

While we waited for the new commercial stations to get organized and on the air, we were getting ready ourselves. We had to build a "make shift" speech studio so that both Japanese and Chinese messages could be recorded for broadcast by shortwave from Far East Broadcasting Company in Manila. (An interesting sidelight on FEBC; one of the co-founders, John Broger, was a navy buddy of mine and now we were working together again, but this time spreading the Gospel of Christ to the Far East.) The shortwave broadcasts from Manila brought many letters such as a young man who wrote, "The Bible course you sent me is very good, because I could learn about our Heavenly Father and Christ. It has strengthened my faith. My father died the other day and as our family religion is Buddhist, so was the funeral service, but I refused to bow to my father's casket and my family scolded me. What attitude should a Christian have in this case? Please lead me."

It wasn't until August of 1951, that we went on the air with our first program in Japan. It was called, "Light for a Darkened World." Getting started wasn't easy. During the war, radio had been used by the militarists as a tool for propaganda. "How could anything good come from the radio?" None of the Japanese pastors wanted to get involved. In fact, to some, it was unspiritual even to listen to the radio! So our first speaker was a graduate student who was coached by one our men how to prepare and

Ministry in Japan

deliver a radio message. He stayed with us until he graduated. By then, Rev. Oe, a highly respected pastor from Hiroshima, (eighteen hours from Tokyo) volunteered to be the pastor. He would come once a month to produce a month of programs. The ice had been broken!

We began receiving funds from different sources. Imagine our surprise when gifts started coming from a group in Australia. Their first one was $1,100! This too was a miracle! Response to the program was on the increase. In February, we received over a hundred and fifty letters in response to the broadcasts. Many of these were TB patients or bedridden and had no other source of Light. We were also encouraged by letters from missionaries who said they had converts in their churches that had come because of the radio broadcasts. By November, we were on eleven stations with Yo No Hikari (Light of the World) a fifteen minute weekly broadcast. Truly God was working.

A missionary wrote, "Working out in the districts, I would like to take this opportunity to express our thanks to your radio work. This ministry is much more effective than we at first were willing to admit. I have had many experiences lately that have convinced me of that fact. We also have had the pleasure of baptizing those won through the radio work. One of our most faithful Christians was a listener. The first question he asked me as I opened the door for him was, 'What shall I do in order to get rid of my sin?' This person had never been to a Christian meeting. The Holy Spirit reached him through radio."

During 1953, there were many changes in the radio work. We were on a total of twenty stations that carried the program. Because of the lack of funds, we had to cut down to ten. However, when the funds increased, we were able to go back to fifteen. We had seen a steady increase in correspondence and enrollment had reached 4300 in three Bible courses. The stations were continually raising the price for broadcast time and our ability to

Chapter 3

meet bills had been affected by the decrease in income. There had been a switch in thought – mission boards were starting to be responsible for the broadcasts in their area with letter response being directed to them instead of us. Satan was doing everything he could to thwart the ministry. One day, unbeknown to us, something went wrong with one of our recorders causing a flaw in the programs. One of the stations tried to use this as an excuse to put us off the air. It was only as we prayed that the victory came: none of the stations dropped us.

1954 had been a year of great changes – mostly in personnel. Tom Watson went to Korea to manage TEAM's radio station, and Art Seely went on furlough. Pastor Oe, who had been our radio speaker, said he could no longer carry that responsibility. The greatest personnel miracle was when Dr. Akira Hatori joined PBA. Where could we have found a man so well educated and knowledgeable in radio, with a heart to reach his own people with the gospel of Jesus Christ? Not to forget, in spite of his poor health, he continued in the ministry for nearly sixty years! (Rev. Oe became a member of our board of trustees.)

Two new programs were added: a thirty minute weekly that ended the year on seven stations, and a children's program – a joint effort with Child Evangelism Fellowship which by the end of the year was on 28 stations. (An interesting sidelight on the children's program called "Children of Light" – airtime was free because we were buying time for an adult program and there were no other children's programs. Another of God's miracles) Our original fifteen minute program was on thirteen stations. We had also started a Korean program, but with TEAM's new station in Korea, we turned that responsibility over to them.

The follow-up ministry continued to grow. We had a total of four correspondence courses which would take two and a half years to complete. Our students ranged in age from fifteen to seventy-five, and we were trying to find a good Bible course for children. Miss Matsumura, the one in charge of our follow-up, became burdened for the contacts who were blind that were responding to the radio programs. She started studying Braille so she could answer their questions. (She was a faithful worker in so many ways.) We found that Emmaus had a complete course in Braille which we could use. At the same time, the Lord led a blind evangelist to join our staff, who became the head of the blind ministry. God's miraculous hand at work again! There was almost nothing being done to reach this segment of the population.

A lesson learned

In 1954, because the Seelys were going on furlough, it was thought that we should bring in a Japanese national to administer so that Jeanette and I could spend time studying the language. The Seelys knew a man about fifty years of age who was experienced in business, but a young Christian. We thought he could fill the position. We all felt this was a step in the right direction of getting the Japanese more involved in the ministry. However, it wasn't long before I had an uneasy feeling about how finances were being handled. One day, Miss Matsumura came to our house and told me that she saw actions being done in the office that were not Christian. She asked me to investigate. What I found wasn't good! We had given too much responsibility to someone that young in the faith to be able to handle. As a result, we found ourselves in debt for thousands of dollars because of the misappropriation of funds! Actually three men were involved, and we had to dismiss all three. This could have destroyed the ministry had it not been for a miracle.

Together with an interpreter, I visited all the stations involved and told them what had happened, and that given time, we would pay all that we owed. God moved the hearts of many missionaries, who sold their cars and other items, and gave the money to

Chapter 3

us to re-coup our financial loss. It was a costly lesson, but in the process it brought about even better relations with the stations.

The Beginning of our church ministry

While busy with the radio ministry, God laid a peculiar burden on our hearts for the people of our area. We did not have the language yet, but we knew that God wanted us to move ahead anyway. Jim and Ruthe Frens, who lived about ten minutes from us, felt the same way we did. They found a church in the area where they lived and decided to visit the next Sunday. But in Jim's words, "We were dumbfounded to be greeted not by a congregation of worshipers, but by rows of tables displaying a variety of things for sale. It was bazaar day!" Later Jim stumbled on to a garden house. It was called Morning Glory Gardens, a well known location because they grew special morning glories; some even for the Emperor. We were able to rent the building for a thousand yen a month ($3.30 in those days.)

Our next step was to ask another missionary, who had a truck equipped to show movies and a good sound system, to help us with a street meeting at the railroad station near the building Jim had rented. After showing the movie and preaching a message, the people were invited to Morning Glory Gardens. (Everybody knew where that was.) The next day was Sunday, and a crowd of over a hundred attended. The following Saturday night, we did the same in our neighborhood, and again we had a good turn out with several being saved. Because of its location, it became known as Morning Glory Church. That was November of 1950. Today the most faithful members in the church are those who were saved in one of those two meetings. Shortly after that, Jim and Ruthe moved to Shizuoka to do church planting. But we were joined by a wonderful couple, Don and Mary McAlpine. (Jim and Ruthe Frens and Don and Mary McAlpine became our best friends-- aunts and uncles to our children.)

Ministry in Japan

Suddenly in 1952, Morning Glory Gardens went bankrupt and offered the church first choice of any portion of the 2000 tsubo (one tsubo is 36 square feet) before it would be sold for a subdivision. We took the option and purchased 175 tsubo for $3,500 and the building for $1,600. The church paid 20% of the cost.

The church began to grow because many missionaries who had English Bible classes brought their contacts to the church on Sundays. In addition to other activities, we had two Bible based plays. Jeanette wrote the first play and the youth leaders did the second one including the costumes. What mother could resist seeing her little cherub performing on stage? In addition, they were hearing the Gospel. The most successful of our special meetings were held in tents. People seemed less reluctant to enter a tent than a church building. One of the greatest joys of our tent meetings was to see our young people at work for the Lord as they welcomed people at the door, passed out tracts, and some were praying outside the tent that people would be saved. Praise the Lord, Morning Glory Church was one of the fastest growing churches in Tokyo. We had about 150 children in Sunday School as well as 100 adults in the morning service.

Because all the preaching was being done by interpretation, we felt it would be helpful if they could have a Japanese pastor come

Chapter 3

once a month to speak and counsel any who had questions. So in 1952, we engaged the services of Kiichi Ando Sensei (teacher) fromFukushima Ken. He continued with us until 1955. There is an interesting sidelight to this arrangement. Pastor Ando would eat with us when he came. One day Paul, who was around four and adding new words to his English vocabulary, was watching him eat. Of course Pastor Ando was eating in the usual Japanese way, slurping the food which was perfectly polite in Japanese society. Paul looked at him and said in English, "Pastor Ando, you're *important!*" Of course, what Paul was trying to say was, "You're *impolite!*" You can be sure we let the matter pass!

It was almost as though we were saying, "Good bye" when we resigned official responsibility from Morning Glory Church on July 26, 1953. It meant that the heavy responsibility of the church would not be on our shoulders, but we would continue to attend services and bring contacts into the church. As the responsibility of the radio ministry was increasing, and the need to study the language continued, we felt it was the right thing to do. The responsibility of the church was now in the very capable hands of the McAlpines. Attendance was averaging about 100 and 50 had followed the Lord in baptism. About that time, it was felt the old garden house needed remodeling to make it more useable for church functions. This made it possible to hold a crowd of 175 and with curtains it could be divided into Sunday school rooms.

We praise the Lord for what He was doing for Morning Glory Church in 1954. He was teaching the church about giving. At this time they were giving 10% of all offerings to the radio ministry, 10% to home missions, 10% to tract follow-up, and 10% to foreign missions. They also undertook a large project of putting a tract in every house in Suginami Ward. Working every Saturday and Sunday afternoon, it took them nine months to complete the project.

Hiroshima - Bernie

It was August, 1950, the fifth anniversary of the dropping of the atomic bomb on Hiroshima. Dr. Fred Jarvis, Dr. David Hesselgrave, and I decided to be there for the occasion to take

Chapter 3

advantage of the opportunity for evangelism. I loaded the Carry-all with tracts, Gospel of Johns, New Testaments, movie projector, and a sound system. For five days we traveled over narrow dirt roads, taking advantage of opportunities each night to gather a crowd to show the Japanese movie, "God of Creation," which had been given to us by Howard Butt, to give out tracts, and to preach through an interpreter who was with us.

We were shocked with what we saw when we arrived! There were people walking on the streets with scars, and bandages, the result of the bomb. It was especially heart rendering as we visited the hospital where the most serious were treated. Another shock awaited us when we arrived at the church where we were staying when a policeman knocked at the door and asked whose vehicle with a sound system was parked in front of the church?

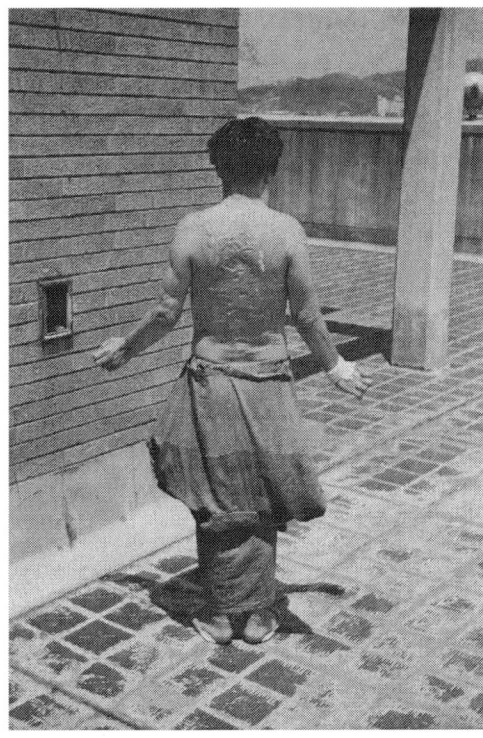

Ministry in Japan

Because the police did not have a vehicle with a sound system, they asked if we would drive them through the city to announce that there would be no public meetings -- except where this vehicle was! What a miracle! After five days of meetings throughout the city, we had distributed almost all our literature. One more note of praise, two prostitutes that had attended one of our street services were saved. We pooled our funds and bought them out of slavery. (In those days prostitution was legal and if any tried to escape, the police would search for them and bring them back.) They both went north to a Bible school and became fruitful followers of the Lord. God was in the miracle working business.

The Visit of Dr. Bob Jones, Sr.

We were also blessed by the visit of Dr. Bob Jones, Sr in 1951. I had arranged his whole itinerary and drove him to all his engagements. Many were saved in the meetings.

He said he had never seen such hungry hearts. I had arranged an interview with General MacArthur, but before it could happen, President Truman recalled him. What a disappointment! When

MacArthur left Japan, people several deep lined the entire 25 mile route to the airport to bid him farewell.

Our move and our family - Jeanette

By early 1952, our family had moved to larger quarters, typically Japanese with straw mats and paper covered doors separating the rooms and hallway. The long hallway had sliding glass doors which could be protected by sliding wooden shutters in case of a typhoon or heavy rain storms.

I really did not want a cat, but one day a man appeared at our door looking for a home for one of those little creatures. Before I could say, "No," to his request, Karen and Paul came to the door and said, "Oh! Isn't he cute?" Of course you know who won that battle! Paul gave him the name, "Ta Chan." He turned out to be

a very lazy cat. There was a little shelf above the refrigerator that was a nice warm spot. He would jump up there and sleep all day long. One day we got some catnip which we thought would make him happy. He took one sniff and jumped back up to his shelf and never went near the catnip again. Once in awhile he would get a spurt of energy and would jump through the paper doors leaving us with a mending job!

In front of our new home was a little pond with an island in the middle. There was a small Shinto shrine on the island where people in the neighborhood would come to worship and burn incense. It was a constant reminder of the darkness that prevails in this land!

The Dance of the gods

People would visit this shrine daily, clap their hands, and beat their drums. It never failed to stab our hearts. At the time of one of Japan's fall festivals, before we realized what was happening, a man with a hideous mask did a dance in front of our house to drive the evil spirits away, and then was angry because we refused to pay him for it. Of course, we explained that we were Christians and could not support what he was doing. Then he returned a second time angrier than ever. Both our helper and interpreter were afraid to go to the door!

The little Holritzes - Jeanette

If our children ever felt any lack of privilege by living in Japan versus in the U.S., we never sensed it. They were making friends with the children in our neighborhood and picking up Japanese phrases that even we did not know. We had some friends by the name of Takamizu. *Mizu* in Japanese means "water," so Paul would jokingly call them "Takawater San." I had found a toy record player before we left the States which would play "Rusty in Orchestraville" teaching them the different instruments in the orchestra as well as nursery rhymes like "The Muffin Man" etc. Often we would be without electricity and Paul, who didn't understand this electric bit, would pray, "Lord bless the plug ins and help them to work." He had a large rubberized duck which he called his "Christian duck" and tried to teach him to pray!

Karen also had a life size doll that she tried to teach proper manners and even Scripture verses she had learned during our family devotions. Whenever any of their toys needed repairs, Bernie was called and asked to "fik it, Daddy." Karen made a number of Japanese friends and was very earnest in asking them to come with her to Sunday school. She would round them all up and remind them to bring a Japanese coin for the offering. Some of the missionaries jokingly said, "She's a good Baptist." Karen was saved when she was five and was our little theologian. One day she asked Jeanette, "Jesus washed my sins away when I was saved, but what about my new sins?"

Karen was now 6 years old and in the second grade. We took Paul (4 years old) to the opening day of school, but the only way the teacher could get his attention was when was she announced it was time for lunch! He immediately stood at attention and marched out with the rest of the students. Shortly after that, we were eating dinner with one of our missionary families. They had a little girl that admired Karen who was older than she. This led the little girl's father to say to Karen, "You are her idol!" That just broke Karen's heart as we had preached against idols and to think that she would be someone's idol was more than she could bear. It was only after much explaining, that she felt better about the whole situation. Such is life on the mission field!

Also of delight to us as well as for the children's creativity, there were no greeting cards in Japan, so they made their own. Many of them we still have and treasure, especially the one that Paul made when he was older was an exact replica of the *Time Magazine* with his dad being "The Man of the Year."

Christmas

There never was a busier city than Tokyo at Christmas time. Since the war, Christmas had become a big celebration; tree decorations and bright lights were everywhere. And since they have no Christ, they make much of Santa Claus. In fact, many thought he is one of the Christian's gods! We appreciated that many of our supporting churches sent Christmas cards. We took the cover off the cards, put them on construction paper, and added Scripture verses about Christ, which delighted our Sunday school children. We are also thankful for the churches that sent packages. One of the packages for Paul contained a pullover sweater with an ornamental football attached to it. Paul did not look at the sweater, he just took hold of the football and said, "Oh look! A football!" We asked Karen to write a thank you letter to the churches. She thanked them profusely and added, "My stockings are wearing out and my dresses are getting old." Then we told her that was not the proper way to write a thank you letter!

The Revival- Bernie

It was April, 1953, when the TEAM missionaries met in Morning Glory Church for their spring prayer conference (it was the largest available hall in our area) but what was to happen was different than before. This was a discouraged, and disheartened group. For all the effort that was put forth, we had little to show for it. But more insidious than that, there was a critical spirit that prevailed. The first day of the conference the speaker was Dr. Good, one of the China missionaries that had come to Japan. Being a doctor he spoke of an illness in which the organs of the body fighting against each other instead of working together. He likened it to what was going on in our midst.

The next day Tom Watson spoke on "Precious in the eyes of the Lord is the death of His saints," comparing it to the need of our dying to self. The third day Dr. Fred Jarvis was the speaker. Partway through his message he stopped to ask forgiveness of one the missionaries he had gossiped about. Then he continued with his message for a while but stopped again and asked another missionary's forgiveness for things he had said about him. Then one of the missionaries in the audience suggested that we stop the meeting and allow time for those who needed to ask forgiveness of others, and a wonderful revival broke out with tears of repentance flowing freely. This began a time of prayer and fasting that spread to other missions. Missionaries would gather all over Tokyo to pray for one another and for revival in the Japanese church. It was the beginning of a new missionary life with more love for each other and the Japanese to whom we had come to minister. One phrase that was heard often was, "I love you, brother." Ten years later, when we heard that phrase, we knew the revival wasn't over!

Our First Major Earthquake

One morning at about 3 a.m. we were literally shaken out of bed; an earthquake as violent as the one that hit Tokyo in 1923 killing many people. We had felt at least a dozen stiff quakes since coming to Japan, but nothing like this one. After a few rumblings, we sat up in bed and began to pray, and then one terrific quake sent us scurrying to the children's room. We all huddled under a safe place. As the epic center was off the coast, damage wasn't too severe. Throughout the day there were after shocks, but none as intense as the first one.

Tragedy

A native believer was killed by a truck. Dwight Bennett was with him when it happened, and miraculously escaped death. The young man was part of a team of Bible school students that was helping Dwight hold evangelistic tent meetings in the country. Dwight called Bernie for help. He returned at 2 a.m. with the body in a box in the back of our Carry-all and left early for Maebashi with the body where the funeral services would be held. What a sad experience to deliver the dead son to his parents. (The only way a corpse can be shipped in Japan is that the coffin be placed in a coach by itself and the fare was charged for all the empty seats!)

Some real Jewels - Jeanette

Kitao and Fumiko Iwasaki were wealthy people with a thriving business in Shanghai, but they lost everything when they had to flee during the war. They returned to Japan, but could never get established as they were in China. Mrs. Iwasaki felt she had to find a job in order to help her children through school. She heard the Holrtizes needed a maid. (I never called her a maid but rather a helper.) Mrs. Iwasaki and I started to read the Bible together – she in Japanese and I in English. We learned from our interpreter that Mrs. Iwasaki thought that even though she had graduated from a well known home economics school, she still did not have enough education to be a Christian. Little did we realize what would transpire in the next few months.

Mrs. Iwasaki soon started attending our church. The first time she visited, she realized she needed Jesus as her Savior. Unlike other Japanese husbands, Mr. Iwasaki did not forbid his wife to go to church, but firmly said, "Don't ever try to get me to believe that myth." Then he came to church a few times to see the foreigners. One Sunday morning, I said to Bernie, "Shall we invite the whole family over for dinner if Mr. Iwasaki is there?" We agreed that we wouldn't say anything about the Lord Jesus on their first visit.

Thankfully the whole family came that Sunday, and Bernie had no more than finished the prayer for dinner when Mr. Iwasaki said, "Will you tell me what has happened to my wife? She has changed so much." As he and Bernie talked about the Lord, Mrs. Iwasaki and Jeanette went into another room to pray. When they came back, Bernie said, "I want to introduce you to our new brother in Christ." Then we saw something that we had never seen in Japan before, as they very seldom show emotion in public. Mr. Iwasaki put his arms around his wife and they wept together. We thank the Lord that not only was a soul saved, but a

home as well. There are very few Christian homes in Japan. Mr. Iwasaki became a leader in our church, in the literature work, and eventually in the radio ministry.

To us, this was one of the greatest miracles we experienced while in Japan. It wasn't only that they established a Christian home, but our families became life long friends. We often had meals at each other's homes. Their son, Akio, said on one occasion, "My mother can't speak English, and Mrs. Holritz speaks very little Japanese, and yet when they are together they 'Yak Yak' all the time." Thank the Lord for the power of the gospel that can change hearts and minds so much.

Mrs. Iwasaki's Testimony

One of our supporting churches wanted a testimony of one of the believers. We asked Fumiko Iwasaki if she would be willing to do so and she consented. It is as follows:

"I praise the Lord for saving me. Before I was saved, I trusted in myself and believed I could do anything by my own efforts. Now I realize that such thinking was due to my own pride and lack of fear of God.

"My father died when I was a child, but I was able to finish high school; and to graduate from a well known home economics school. Later I went to Shanghai to marry my fiancé who had established himself in a very successful business in that country. But after the war, we Japanese were forced to return to Japan, and we lost our beautiful home and all our savings. Back in Japan, we started life over again. These were very hard years, but finally my husband was able to build up a good business once more, only to have it fail later and all his friends turned against him. My husband worked hard as he was anxious to provide for his family the way he had in previous years, but the harder he tried the more difficult things became.

"Through these years, I came to feel I needed something besides myself and my own human strength to carry me through, but little did I realize that need was God and His Son, Jesus Christ.

"It was difficult to come to the decision that I should find a job for myself, but I wanted our children to be able to continue their education in one of the better, private schools of Japan. Then it was that I heard I could get a job working for a missionary. When I came to work for Mr. and Mr. Holritz, and began to observe their daily lives, I came to realize that spiritual things were more important than material things. Shortly after I began helping them, in Jan. 1954, I trusted Christ as my Savior.

"Since I have been saved, I have had a most wonderful answer to prayer. After praying for some months and believing the promises of I Cor. 7:13-16 and Acts 16:31, my husband, who had said he could not believe the myth of Jesus Christ and who walked on the road to eternal destruction, was saved. Now I am amazed that God has answered my prayer, for though I was praying for him, it seemed like an impossible thing. But praise God all things are possible with Him. I have confidence that God works in us as the living God.

"I can't explain how great our joy is since our salvation. My husband and I were baptized in January, 1955, and many of our true friends, our brothers and sisters in Christ, came to our baptismal service. It's so wonderful that now my husband and I are one in the Lord, and we and our three children can read the Bible together each day. Before, we had nothing in common, but now God and His Word are the center of our thinking, Eph. 5:8 is what God has done for us, and we want to grow in Jesus Christ and live for the glory of God.

"When I think of our past lives, I am thankful that my husband's business failed for if it hadn't, I am sure that I would never have come to know about redemption through Jesus Christ on the cross. I thank the Lord for Mr. and Mrs. Holritz who led us to Christ. I pray that God will bless them MUCH as they have devoted themselves to the evangelizing of Japan and have been working very hard fighting many difficult battles in this difficult country.

"In closing, I praise the Lord that though you are Americans and I am Japanese, I can call you my brothers and sisters in the Lord.

Fumiko Iwasaki"

OUR FAMILY'S FIRST FURLOUGH 1955 ~ 1957

The Phenomenon of Furlough - Bernie

I call it a phenomenon because in the ordinary work force you don't have a furlough, you have a vacation. In the military you have a furlough and it is a vacation. But to the missionary a furlough is a vacation of a sort, but it is much more. There is the need to visit family and friends as well as the churches and individuals that have been the source of your support as well as the project ministry in which you may have been involved. There may be the need of further education. For some it may mean the need of special medical attention. Thus for these reasons missions do not refer to this time as a furlough but "A Home Assignment" as there are specific goals that are to be reached before returning to the field.

With that introduction, we'd like to share with you what we did on our first furlough. On August 28, 1955, we boarded the freighter, *China Transport*, to return to the States for furlough. All the Holritz family had been looking forward to this day, that is with the exception of our little six year old Paul, who had heard from another little missionary's child (who had never been to the States) that America was full of wild buffaloes! However, we had told him so many wonderful stories about the U.S. we wondered if he was out to prove his school buddy wrong. You never can tell what a six year old might be thinking. Our trip back was smooth sailing all the way, so we spent much of the time out on the deck. From time, to time we would walk up to the forecastle of the ship and watch the porpoises swim as if racing with the ship. We even saw hammerhead sharks.

One very interesting thing happened a day before we were to arrive in San Francisco. There were some girls coming from China, and they had brought a delicacy with them intending to share with their friends in San Francisco. However, the steward said that their "one hundred year old eggs" would not get through customs. If they didn't want to throw them away, they should eat them before arriving. How glad we were that they chose to eat them out on the deck. The smell was horrible!

Jeanette

We were met by Hideo Aoki of the Japanese Evangelical Mission Society with whom Akira Hatori was associated. He took us to lunch and then showed us around the sites before we were to catch the train for LA where Bernie's brother and his family lived. We had several wonderful days with them visiting Disney World and other sites before we boarded the train in LA for the long trip to Corpus Christi, TX. After setting in our seats, I was occupied with staring out the window hoping not to miss any of the houses and country side as well as the many cars. (Japan had not yet come into its own in the automobile industry.) When we arrived in Corpus Christi, my family was there to meet us. Evidently I had lost most of my southern drawl. I turned to Bernie and said, "Did I ever sound like that?!" Our children were good travelers, however, they were always inquisitive about the next friend's house where we would stay, "Do they have any kids and do they have any toys?" We had fun as a family by making up games to play such as finding letters of the alphabet on bulletin boards. The only time Karen got a little irked was when her daddy hit a bump while she was drinking water. Her response was, "You spilled my water, Daddy!"

We were at the Church of the Open Door in Greenville, Mississippi, during their VBS, and Paul, returning home from one of the sessions said, "I'm so tickled about something, Mother." And I said, "What about, Son?" He replied, "I just got saved and I'm so tickled I don't know what to do!" My reply was, "That is wonderful; go and tell your Daddy as he will want to know."

Since we returned to the States in August 1955, we were busy visiting churches, friends, and family, as well as our mission's annual conference. Between May 16 and July 20, 1956, we were in 16 states raising support for ourselves and for PBA. We left Winnipeg for meetings in North Dakota through the month of August. After that, we had invitations in other states, but needed guidance as to which churches we should accept.

Radio Work in Japan - Bernie

Word from Japan stated that the broadcast ministry was at its most effective peak. Surveys indicated a potential listening audience of between five and six million people. No wonder then, that a great variety of evil forces were arrayed against us; and that the few individuals who produced the programs would be subject to attacks. Our hearts were always heavy when we heard of another program being taken off the air. The time was Jan. 1956; the place: the center of Shintoism in Japan; the reason: no funds to keep it on the air!

We also learned that Akira and his wife, Reiko, were both in a TB sanitarium. With the burden to win his own people to the Lord, was it any wonder that Satan was doing all he could to keep him from it? At the same time, the building that housed the studio we occasionally used for recordings was made available to rent. Up until this time our offices were scattered in different missionary homes, but now we could all be together in one location and have a recording studio of our own. The different ingredients for the daily broadcast were coming together but we needed finances and prayer support.

There were thirty-five stations carrying our programs by the end of 1956 when we received word from a church in the States saying they were interested in taking on the support of another station. In addition Loran McCall, a missionary already on the field, volunteered to join us in the engineering department, taking some of the load that Bernie Shaw was doing alone. By the end of the year, we were encouraged: new workers had joined the staff, a new member was elected to the board of directors, progress was being made with the government towards incorporation, and funds had come in enabling us to buy some urgently needed equipment. We were even able to lay the foundation for our own studio building.

Preparations to return to Japan

In January 1957, we moved to San Francisco to a place that housed missionaries going to or returning from the mission field called Home of Peace. They helped the missionaries with purchases at lower prices as well as providing space and material to pack and crate for shipment to the mission field. There were about forty of us counting children. By now we had moved the children to eight different schools! When we arrived in San Francisco, Karen & Paul said, "We don't want to go to another school until we get back to Japan!" It had been a hard year for them and we understood their feelings.

OUR SECOND TERM 1957 ~ 1962

Back to Japan

Funds had come in for equipment, passage, and support. The mission gave the "go ahead" and the ship on which we had hoped to sail which had canceled once opened up again, and we rebooked passage. We were delighted to have the Dwight Bennett family as our fellow passengers. It proved to be THE TRIP NEVER TO BE FORGOTTEN! On Feb. 25, 1957, at dusk the gangplank was hoisted, and the 7,500 ton freighter, China Bear, slowly pulled away from the wharf. What joy to be on our way back to Japan!

Ministry in Japan

Watching the lights of San Francisco fade in the distance we sang "I have decided to follow Jesus... No turning back, No turning back." Joy filled our hearts as we thought of the way God had so wondrously provided for our needs to return to the field of our calling.

We experienced almost every kind of weather - hail, snow, high winds, storms, and tidal waves from an earthquake, all during the last week of our trip. At that time of year, storms lurk everywhere on the high seas and, though praise God, we missed the center of some very bad ones, we felt their effects. We saw several ton of three quarter inch steel sheets lashed by the winds and waves, finally cut loose from their heavy chains on the deck of

Chapter 3

the ship and slide overboard! One would never know how much a ship could shake or roll almost to the point of no return unless he had experienced it!

Arriving safely in Japan we learned from the captain what the real danger had been. The fact that $100,000 worth of steel had been lost was the least of their worries. He said, "The steel sheets dashing back and forth by the waves had already started to cut into the hatches, and I thought I had lost my ship." All the crew had been alerted and we would have had help in two hours from another ship. One does not like the thought of getting into one of those midget life boats in rough waters to get to another ship. Neither was the thought of losing all our freight (beds, refrigerator, groceries etc.) which people had sacrificed to give us. The sweetest thing about the trip to all of us was the perfect calm and peace we had in our hearts at all times. There were occasions when we couldn't eat very well nor sleep because of being tossed about so much, but never were any of us, including the children, the least bit afraid. We believe the fact that we arrived safely with our baggage was an answer to prayers.

It was with joy we reached land March 13, after 16 days on the water – four days longer than our first trip to Japan. We had to

leave our ship and come in to the dock on a motor launch. Our ship carried explosives and the U.S. Army felt it too risky for our ship to come into the harbor. You never know what kind of cargo these freighters may have on board! We were thrilled to be met by Japanese and missionary friends, but were sorry that some of them left before we could take their pictures. Bernie isn't in the picture either as he was occupied with custom officials. We were glad to walk up and down the narrow streets of Japan once more, to visit the tiny, dingy shops, and somehow, we don't even mind the smell of the fish markets! A CONFIRMATION THAT GOD HAS CALLED US TO THIS LAND!

Chapter 3

First Impressions

Our trip to Shimizu to see the Frens which took three hours added impetuous to our call to the radio ministry. As we were looking out the window practically the entire time, not once did we see a church! There were crowds wherever we went. We saw a house with a large wreath of blue and white paper flowers which marked the home where someone had died. The government reports there are two thousand deaths a day in Japan! Most of these people stepped into eternity without Christ – LOST! We were seeing the enemy continuously taking more and more into his camp. The night we arrived at the Frens, they took us out into their backyard. Across the street was a large shrine. Some fifty or sixty people were chanting in unison to their gods. This is a new religion (Soka Gakkai) which has included doctrines from all the other religions of the land - including Christianity and has also become a political party. We were awakened the next morning at about 4:30, by the chants of these people. Ezekiel 37 talks of "an open valley full of dry bones." This was a perfect picture of what we saw in Japan. Most of these people would never see a missionary or pastor, but our hope was to reach them by radio!

Back to language school – Again!

One day the Lord opened an opportunity to witness in the class. There were three missionary ladies, an army fellow and a Nisei (a Japanese not born in Japan) in our class. Neither the army man nor the Nisei were Christians. Every hour we had a different teacher. In the second hour, it so happened we had a teacher for whom we had been praying. As soon as he came into class he said, "When we read the basic sentences from our book and I ask the question, 'Do you go to movies?' you three ladies always say, 'No.' Now I would like for you to carry on a discussion in Japanese to the rest of the class explaining why you don't go to the movies." The Lord really helped us, and we were able to give our reasons clearly. When we finished, the teacher turned to the Nisei (who was quite a playboy) and said, "Well, Oshima San, it would be a good idea if you became a Christian and me too." As a result of that little discussion, the door was opened for Bernie to talk with both the teacher and the Nisei, Oshima San, who listened intently.

Radio - Bernie

We were able to purchase part of the land that houses our office and makeshift studio and lay the foundation for the new studios. The radio stations took surveys in 1958 to ascertain the listening audience of their programs. From a recent report, we learned we had a potential listening audience of between five and six million people who listened to one of our three programs. These broadcasts were sponsored by 13 different groups or individuals on 48 stations weekly. That means the cost of giving the gospel to one person 52 times in the year was ONE CENT! What a door the Lord had opened to proclaim the gospel in this land. It was amazing to see the willingness of so many stations to make such inviting offers to help us put our programs on their stations. Much prayer and money was needed to take advantage of their proposals.

We were thankful for the makeshift studio we had in the building we were renting, but it had terrible weaknesses. Can you imagine the frustration of being in the middle of producing a program and an airplane flies overhead, or someone in the offices upstairs opens a drawer, drops a book, slides a chair, or someone comes into the building, or even a truck drives by, and the program having to be re-done? We needed to finish building our soundproof studios soon. In May, we received word from the director of Far Eastern Gospel Crusade that a church on the east coast was interested in raising funds for a building program on the mission field. He asked us to submit our plans for the studio building! That church selected our project and sent a check for $2,200 enabling us to put up the walls, the roof, and install all the complicated wiring. Then came word from Back to the Bible Broadcast that they too would like to have a part in the construction of our studio. By God's grace, we believed we could have it completed by the end of the year.

On Christmas Day, the workers of PBA (missionaries and nationals with their families) had dinner together. We had sukiyaki, a Japanese variety of beef stew, with a kind of noodle which you can't possibly chew. We nicknamed them "rubber bands" but it

was a very delicious meal and we liked it, rubber bands and all! As we were together, we were reminded of what God had done for PBA through the years. A few years ago, we were only on a few stations and just a hand full of personnel. Now our group had expanded and there were around 50 counting the wives and children.

The burden we had for so many years had at last become a reality. On January 26, 1959, our first daily program went on the air in the city of Osaka – a city about the size of Chicago. The Lord had performed some miracles in this venture: God raised up a sponsor, and the station dropped the price. The second day the program was on the air, another station called, and wanted us to

Ministry in Japan

air the program on their station too, but we didn't have the funds to do so. The Lord moved in, and the station said that because they already had our weekly program, they would give us six months free time for the daily program while we looked for a sponsor!

In 1960, Akira and Reiko Hatori went on furlough for a year. He spoke at a conference in London and then made a survey trip to South America to see where the Japanese were to help determine where the signal from HCJB should be beamed in order to reach them. There are over one million Japanese in South America. One of the PBA staff, Kazuo Ozaki, had gone to HCJB to oversee the Japanese broadcasts.

Bernie and two of the staff made a ten day trip to the northern part of Japan to visit eight different TV stations and record programs using local church personnel. It was encouraging to see the improvement in their musical ability. During the war, there was no music taught in the schools, and the effects were still seen.

Our hearts were thrilled to see the large music studio finished, enabling us to do ALL our recordings in our own studios as well as the duplication of programs for distribution to all the radio stations. For the previous two years, we had to rent other studios in different parts of Tokyo and transport expensive pieces of equipment. We had waited ten years for this to become a reality. It was a great miracle; the result of the sacrifice of many churches and individuals overseas, missionaries, missions, and a number of Japanese Christians.

We had been working with the Japanese government for the past year to be registered as a "legal juridical institution." There had been many battles, but at last it was complete. In order that the name of the organization in English be the same as it was in Japanese, it was changed to Pacific Broadcasting Association (PBA).

For some time, we had been conscious of the Lord's leading to prepare a Christian children's program. There were eighteen million children in Japan and not one Christian children's broadcast. Neither were there any Christian music records. These were the two main goals we wanted to accomplish in 1961.

For a long time we had been praying for a piano. When Prairie Bible Institute heard of the need, They raised $750. After talking to two piano companies, we realize that was just half of what we needed. One of the staff noticed an announcement that a missionary was selling a grand piano of the type we needed with a sale price of $790! When they heard that we were interested, they lowered the price to $750. Margaret Halberg, our pianist, looked it over and was well satisfied. The next day the piano was moved to our studio; a wonderful answer to prayer.

A new opportunity came to us. A five minute daily spot at midnight on a 50,000 watt station in Tokyo previously used by Seventh Day Adventists became available. At that time of night, their signal is heard over all the islands of Japan. It is also the time when students listen to radio. A sponsor in Australia was interested in taking on its support.

Ministry in Japan

The previous year we began an outreach of visiting churches in the area with a team from PBA to have radio rallies in their area and challenge them to use radio and TV as tools for evangelism. Over 400 came to know Christ through these rallies. We also produced two Christmas TV programs in 1962 for Don McAlpine of TEAM in Nagano city. There were 240 contacts and attendance at his church had increased. After that he signed a ten week contract with the station.

We were able to film the Easter programs and make them available to churches and for other special occasions. But it was not without incident! Satan opposed the whole way. The studio where the filming was to be produced was constantly changing their agreement. On the day the program was to be made, a strike was called. But the Lord intervened, and they filmed the program anyway. As Bernie was helping unload the organ from the truck, he bent over to pick up something, and the end gate fell on his head! He spent two weeks in bed with a brain concussion, but it was worth all the effort. Six stations, including Tokyo, carried the message of the resurrected Christ. Individual missionaries and mission boards raised the money to make this special program possible.

Chapter 3

Relocation and growth of the Church - Bernie

In 1957, when the McAlpines returned from furlough, the attendance had dropped to about fifty. It was decided to sell the property in Eifukucho and move to Meidaimae, an intersection of two railroads. It was also closer to the station thus more accessible. The opening soon came to purchase the new property. The old location was sold to TEAM, and with an additional $1,000, the land was purchased and a new building erected. The church also bought pews and an organ. All of this was done in addition to their monthly giving towards evangelism, foreign mission, tracts, radio, and follow up.

The coming of Junji Hatori as the new pastor was definitely a forward step in the life of the church. It is interesting to note that he had been an avowed communist having been purged during the days of MacArthur, and later was won to the Lord by his brother, Akira. His messages spoke to the hearts of the people and his leadership in the walk of faith sparked another period of growth. When he came, the attendance was down to less than 100 and there were financial difficulties. He challenged them by faith to take the sponsorship of the fifth Sunday radio broadcast on the Tokyo station. Each one yen in the collection would go towards the purchase of tracts, and each Sunday evening they would have a street service.

When I had been teaching the Ten Commandments to a Bible class at Morning Glory Church, I would give an invitation at the end. On one occasion two young men accepted the Lord, but there was another who looked very troubled when we discussed the matter of not bowing to anyone or object other than to God. That presents a problem to the Japanese, as they worship the spirits of their ancestors. He was absent for several weeks. When he finally he came back, the pastor had the joy of leading him to Christ.

In the early days, after we started the church, there was a young man who had been saved in one of the services. Before we left on our first furlough, he had married one of the girls in the church and moved away. He came to the radio office to see Bernie and said he had moved back and was living in a city not far from here. He said there were no churches in the area, so he had started a meeting in his home. He asked Bernie to come and speak from time to time and to help them find a national pastor to lead the church.

It was wonderful to see Morning Glory Church grow and get its own vision of the "field that are white unto harvest" in other parts of the world. For some time, they have been supporting the radio ministry, as well as taking part of the support of a young Japanese pastor who felt called to the Philippines

Someone broke into the home of one of the members of our church and stole some money. When the church found out about it, they prayed for him and took up an offering. It was just a few pennies short of what had been stolen. They were learning to care for one another.

There is always the need to pray for the believers and their walk with the Lord. Because there are so few, we tend to push them forward as examples before an unbelieving world. As a result, they can become a target of Satan. Such is the case of the Iwasaki family. Recently their picture was on the cover of the leading Christian magazine in Japan. Inside was their testimony of how they came to Christ. At Christmas, Mrs. Iwasaki was asked to give her testimony on the radio with almost nationwide coverage. Then Mr. Iwasaki was reelected to the deacon board of the church. Recently their daughter made a profession of faith in Christ. It was a wonderful testimony of God's grace, but also one that the Devil would like to attack.

Chapter 3

One of the biggest battles we face in the Japanese church is the marriage problem. Parents and relatives do the choosing and very seldom consider their son or daughter's plea for a Christian mate. With a strong family loyalty in their background, it is a terrific battle when the young Christian refuses to marry the non-Christian that had been picked out for them. The PBA staff had been praying for three girls in the office who were faced with this problem. But praise the Lord, He gave the victory.

Jeanette's ministry in the Church

After Junji Sensei came to the Church, I had a very close relationship with Toshiko San, his wife. We started a ladies' meeting

and took turns doing the speaking. Of course, she spoke Japanese, but I did not know enough of the language to speak publicly, so she interpreted for me.

I had decided to make cup cakes and cookies for the church's Christmas night fellowship, and thought I would be safe in making 80 as we only had 60 out last year, but there were 140! Those that didn't get cup cakes got cookies. Toshiko San had also made sweet bean soup with little rice balls which was very delicious, so we had plenty. The Japanese do enjoy the home baked goodies as they don't bake in their own homes. At one meeting where Toshiko San was speaking, a little old lady came up to me, handed me a gift of money, and said, "You are such a good cook!" I'm certainly not a gourmet cook, but the Japanese seemed to enjoy my cooking. The ladies always liked the Christmas meetings in our home. We played games, had a devotional, and homemade treats.

When I knew that Mrs. Hatori was expecting, I asked if she would mind if we gave her a baby shower and she seemed delighted. Baby showers were unheard of in Japan at that time. We had brought two life size baby dolls to Japan for Karen. I divided the ladies into two groups to compete with each other.

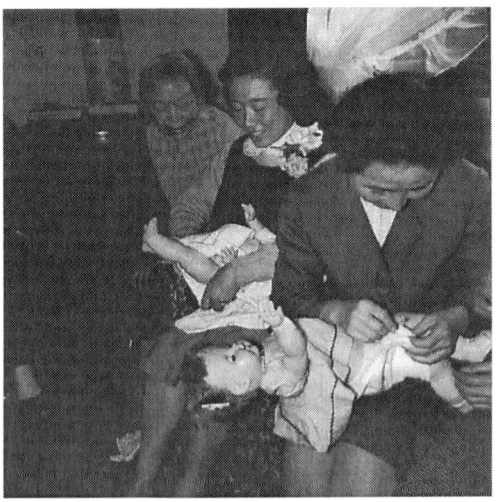

At the beginning of each row, the lady held a baby doll in a diaper and a good sized safety pin. The object was that they were to pretend that Pastor Hatori was calling his wife to hurry as the service was about to begin, but she had to change the baby's diaper before she could go! The lady at the beginning of each row had to take the diaper off, then put it on again, and pass it to the lady next to her. The row that finished first would be the winner. The ladies were hilarious, which made me very happy.

Chapter 3

If I had a ministry gift, it was what the Japanese called "Shokudo Dendo" which means "dinner evangelism". We did not limit our hospitality to believers. If we knew of any who were unbelievers, we would invite them to our house for dinner. I think we were first encouraged in this type of ministry by the visit of the Iwasaki family.

There are two examples that mean so much to me. I think of Mr. and Mrs. Ida, who were not save. (The couple next to Bernie.) Their niece, had been witnessing to them but they would not

respond. Mr. Ida was very belligerent and we were surprised when he accepted our invitation for dinner. They were both gloriously saved that day. About six weeks later Mr. Ida had what they thought was appendicitis. However, when they operated they found his abdomen full of cancer! We were surprised at Mr. Ida, being a new Christian, witnessing to everyone including his relatives. Before his conversion he had been a rogue, but now his relatives could not get over the drastic change. In a few short weeks he passed away. I had Mrs. Ida and some of her friends to our home after the funeral.. She commented how wonderful the fellowship had been, but she said she must go home to take care of her husband's urn. I said to her, "Mrs. Ida, your husband is not in that urn but in heaven with Jesus." At that she brightened up.

The other example is one I treasure the most, because it is an illustration of cooperative evangelism. Mrs. Furuhashi was a dear Christian lady from our church. Her husband was not saved. It was discovered that he had cancer. As soon as we found out about his condition, Bernie and I started carrying food in the car to the entire family. Later, as he was unable to eat solid foods, I made jello, puddings, or soup, and took them on my bike. Then I had an idea and approached Mr. Iwasaki to see if he would write Romans 10:9&10 in his beautiful Japanese Kanji. Finally, one day Mr. & Mrs Furuhashi invited me in, and I left the plaque with him. Mrs. Furuhashi told me later that he had been gloriously saved. Pastor Iide wanted to be sure. He went to visit and found that it was definitely true. While at our mission conference, I heard that he had passed away, so I went back to Tokyo for his funeral.

There were 29 ladies from Morning Glory Church to squeeze into the front room of our house for their annual Christmas party. They had a wonderful time eating and talking. I brought a brief message. When it was all over, one of the ladies asked, "Whatever will we do next year when the Holritzes are on furlough?" Many of the ladies were in their 70's and 80's. One of them was saved earlier and finally her husband, who was older than she, was also saved. Then they started coming to every meeting the church had. Her husband said, "We have waited so late in life to be saved, so now we need to learn lots in a short time, so we come to all the services!"

Life as an MK (Missionary Kid)

The children rode the bus to school everyday. It was more than an hour each way over some very rough roads. They left home at 7:30 and returned at 5, but we were fortunate that our children could live at home. There were some who boarded at the school, and only got to see their parents on the weekends, or holidays. Both continued with their piano lessons and in addition Karen took violin, and Paul cello. Karen also taught an English class to Japanese students. Someone gave us a dog that delighted Karen and Paul, and one day the dog had puppies! They had fun playing with them and then giving them to some of their friends. The children had many Japanese friends to visit, play with and take to church.

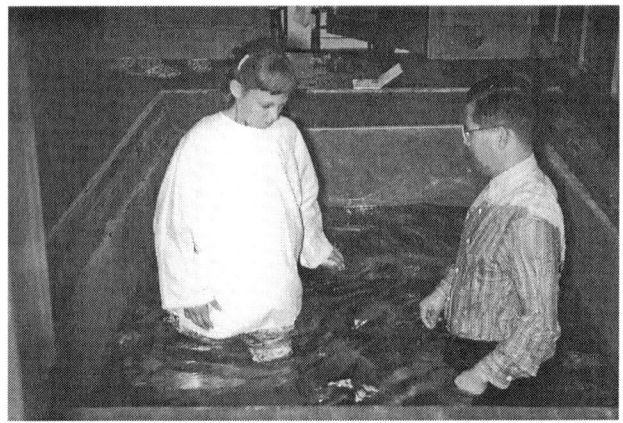

One Easter Sunday, it was a blessing to see both Karen and Paul follow the Lord in baptism and also special to have radio pastor, Akira Hatori, baptize them. We believe it was a testimony to the Japanese, even though they find it difficult to believe that children could be saved. In addition, the oldest Iwasaki boy, Tateo,

was also baptized. He was thirteen, and gave a very clear testimony before the church of how he had been saved at the summer Bible camp.

Family Activity - Jeanette

There were many opportunities to witness. One day we rode home from church on our bikes. As we sped by a lady, she said

in English, "Look, the whole family!" We stopped and I went back to talk to her. She asked the lady where she had learned such perfect English and invited her to church.

We were making an eight hour trip on the train, and the only place to sit was on our suitcases in the vestibule of the coach. At one of the stops, a lady from the first class car ahead of us came walking through the train to get some exercise, and stopped to talk to us. She must have taken some special interest in us as she continued making contact since our first meeting. Her son, who was studying law in Tokyo, came to see us several times. While she was in Tokyo on business she visited us, and brought two Japanese dolls, one for Karen and one for Paul. (The one for

Paul was a sumo wrestler.) Her son came to church with us a couple times and we had witnessed to Mrs. Nagano. We had been praying that family would come to the Lord.

Our children had some very dear friends whom they usually saw in Karuizawa, a place where missionaries sought spiritual and physical refreshment. The Youngquists ministered in Wakayama and we were in Tokyo. We shall never forget our visit to their home in Wakayama. The friendship of the entire family has deepened through the years. When we were returning to Tokyo from our mission conference in Karuizawa, I mentioned to Bernie that I hoped the train wouldn't be as crowded as last year when we took turns sitting on our suitcases in the entrance of the coach for the four hour trip. Then I remembered that Bernie was able to witness to a young fellow all the way to Tokyo and led him to Christ. He has been coming to our church ever since. Praise the Lord.

It was the time for the fall festival. While we sat in church, we heard the parade as well as the drums at the temple. Although we heard this over and over, it never ceased to stab our hearts with pain. God help us never to get hardened to it, but remember that these people are lost and on their way to hell.

Preparations for Furlough - Bernie

The Lord led us to return to the States by way of Europe this time! Meetings were scheduled in Switzerland, Germany, England, and Sweden. The purpose was to challenge the Christians in Europe with the opportunities of radio evangelism in Japan. Plans were to visit missionary radio installations in Hong Kong, Manila, Singapore, Colombo (later called Sri Lanka), and Radio Free Europe in Monaco. Although our ship would take us near the Holy Land, we could not visit there because of the lack of funds. (We supplemented our travel funds with some that

Jeanette received as an inheritance.) We would arrive in the States about the middle of August.

OUR SECOND FURLOUGH 1962 ~ 1963

Our Trip to Europe - Bernie

We left Yokohama on May 23, 1962, aboard the Chusan, a British passenger liner, and the first stop was HONG_KONG. The situation there was heart rendering. A city built to accommodate

800,000 had swelled to 3.2 million! The government was completing one apartment building a week, but still there were thousands living on the street. Besides the radio ministry, we saw the work of the China Boat Mission. Bill Kinkade, a classmate from BJU, showed us around. Imagine, 300,000 people in two small areas averaging five people to a boat together with chickens and dogs: thousands of people and all too few to reach them.

Next we visited the work of Far East Broadcasting Company (FEBC) in MANILA. For years we had wanted to visit this work to which we had been sending taped programs. It was a thrill to see all those huge transmitters wholly dedicated to the proclamation of the Gospel to the Far East. (We were thankful to get back on the ship in one piece! I don't think there were any rules for driving cars there!)

SINGAPORE is one big beautiful garden. However, beautiful gardens, buildings, and modern roads cannot cover the spiritual darkness and cruel heathen rites. There was complete liberty for the Gospel in the free state of Singapore, but not so across the river in Malaya. Witnessing can be done to the Chinese, but not

to the Malaysians who must be Hindu. This was heavy on the hearts of the missionaries. A missionary and a convert had recently been expelled from Malaya.

Our hearts went out to Don Rubesh and the work of Back to the Bible Broadcast in SRI LANKA. A week before we arrived, the last Christian broadcast was taken off Radio Ceylon. The Rubeshes had been producing 25 programs a week, and over the past five years, one by one they had been taken off the air -- the result of militant Buddhism.

Chapter 3

We were only in BOMBAY (called <u>Mumbai</u> now) a few hours so do not have much to report except that we saw the darkness of idolatry everywhere. Bombay's streets are crowded with people and "sacred cows!"

It was Sunday evening when we came to the part of the RED SEA through which Moses led the children of Israel. I had the privilege of preaching to about 30 of the passengers. What a thrill to tell them that the God who delivered the children of Israel from the hand of Pharaoh is the same God who delivers them from the hand of the devil today.

EGYPT is as dry spiritually as are its deserts! The only reason we could get into the countrywas because we were part of the ship's party on tour. We passed through a desert region while we were riding the tour bus en route to CAIRO. There was no vegetation, only sand, sand, and more sand. We saw an old lady dressed in black leading a little boy. It reminded us of Hagar and Ishmael and wondered how they could have existed in such an arid terrain. As part of the tour, we were to ride camels from the bus stop to the pyramids. We were told not to give money to the

guides. However, half way to the pyramids our guide stopped the camels and refused to take us further unless we paid him extra money. It was a scary moment, but finally we were able see the pyramids.

The ship had passed through the Suez Canal by the time the bus got us back. We boarded the ship and headed for Italy. On June 30, five weeks after leaving Yokohama, the Chusan docked in NAPLES. We were met by missionaries from Conservative Baptist Foreign Mission with whom we stayed. The next morning we took the train for Pompeii where we spent a very interesting day.

POMPEII had been a very licentious city! You see this as you visit the excavated displays as well as the murals in the villas that have been uncovered. What happened to the city was as though it were a judgment of God. Without warning Mount Vesuvius erupted, very much like Mount St. Helen a few years back. The ash was so dense and came down so suddenly people were stopped in their tracks; buried right where they were. Pompeii was completely covered with ash and lava and disappeared physically. It was also forgotten for centuries until the early part of the 1900s when it was stumbled upon and excavation began and is still continuing. The figures of both animals and humans were actually cavities in the ash. The remains were disintegrated and what you see now are plaster casts. The gladiator rings, theaters, and baths as well as shops and villas are being uncovered perfectly intact as they were the day the mountain erupted!

From Naples we went to ROME, a city of history. At one time it was the center of the world. As the saying goes, "All roads lead to Rome." Many of the ancient sites are still there to view though much of it is in shambles. As you view the different sites you can't help seeing the magnificence of the ancient city. There are places that are significant to Christians such as the Coliseum, the place where hundreds of Christians were slaughtered by gladiators and animals; The Apian Way, the road that the Apostle Paul was supposed to have walked as he was brought to Rome; the Mamertine Prison where Paul spent his last days on earth; and the miles and miles of catacombs where Christians hid to escape the slaughter that was taking place.

We stayed several days visiting the various historic sights including Vatican City. Paul became very sick and as a result he and Jeanette were unable to visit the catacombs. So Karen and I went alone. We had a very interesting experience in Rome. Jeanette noticed a tour bus and thought she saw the familiar face of a classmate from BJU. She ran over to the bus, and called her name, and sure enough it was she! We had a very unfortunate experience as we were leaving Rome for Monte Carlo - we left Karen's suitcase on the station platform! The station master found it, and turned it over to American Express. It finally caught up with us as we were getting ready to leave Sweden for America, four weeks later!

While in MONTE CARLO, it was challenging to see what Trans World Radio was doing to broadcast the Gospel into Europe, especially the communist countries. A classmate of ours and his

Ministry in Japan

wife were the only ones doing the Russian programs. To think that the building and transmitters were built by Hitler for his propaganda to Africa, and were now dedicated to the proclamation of the Gospel to Europe and Africa!

In the 38 days we were in Europe, I spoke in 28 churches. These meetings were in SWITZERLAND, GERMANY, ENGLAND, and SWEDEN, resulting in some good offerings being sent to Japan and the possibility of sponsorship of some radio programs. Bernie's mother's parents were from Sweden and we were fortunate enough to be able to contact a distant relative, and spend a day with them. However, we were not able to communicate enough to give them the Gospel. God worked a miracle to get us

to the plane that would take us to America. The hotel clerk had given us the wrong information regarding the train that would take us to Guttenberg, the city where we would catch our plane the next day. As a result, we missed the train! But there had been heavy rains during the night that had washed out the tracks north and east of us which forced the express train to be re routed through the town where we had our last meeting. Thus we were able to catch our plane that landed us in New York on August 9.

Furlough in the State - Jeanette

We had a wonderful reunion with Bernie's family in Winnipeg. This is the first time the family has been together in 22 years! From there, we traveled to Greenville, SC, to be near one of our supporting churches. The Lord graciously provided a way for our children to attend Bob Jones Academy, which they enjoyed immensely. We spent a month cleaning and repairing an old two room house we rented. On Dec. 10, Bernie finished three months of practical TV training at one of the local stations, which would be of help when we returned to Japan. All these activities had managed to keep us busy.

We started our deputation meetings when Bernie finished his TV course. We were in Greenville, Miss, Feb. 13 – 17, 1963; Houston, TX, March 9-17, our mission's conference in Elmhurst, IL, May 15-19. Then we moved to TX for the month of June. Whenever we were in Texas, we would be sure to visit the Red McSpaddens who, along with their sweet children, became our very dear friends. We are looking forward to meeting Red in heaven as he has gone on ahead of us. We were in North Dakota for the month of July then on to the west coast until we sailed for Japan.

Ministry in Japan

Preparation to return to Japan

We were in contact with our mission for a sailing date in August, but were advised that transportation funds and monthly support would have to be in hand one month in advance of sailing or we would have to cancel the date. We were hoping not to be delayed anymore for the sake of the children's schooling, as well as the work on the field. The dead-line passed and we were faced with the decision as to whether we could make the Sept. 19th sailing date. As this was the busy season of the year, the shipping company called our mission saying they needed to know ten days earlier than usual whether we would be able to make our sailing date. Because passage, equipment money, and support were so low, we were advised to cancel that reservation date also! That was hard as it completely changed our plans. Finding another sailing date could possibly change our port of debarkation which would mean finding other housing and the children would have to register in another school. We felt like Abraham when it says of him, "He went out not knowing whither he went!"

It would be nice to say that we had not been discouraged. But one Sunday morning, the Lord spoke to us by a message from another missionary. The point was we should look forward WITH ANTICIPATION to each trail that God allows to come into our lives to see how He was going to bring about the solution.

Our support had been raised, and enough gifts had come in to enable us to pay for our steamship tickets, but there was nothing to pay for freight, customs, and inland transportation. This was also true of our outfit needs. We had been in contact with our mission, and they advised us to go anyway and pay back what we had to borrow as quickly as we could. We had not done anything like that before, but felt no restraint from the Lord. With the new schedule, we had to have all our packing done and on the dock in Los Angeles, by October 11. The temperature the last three days had been 106 making it hard to do anything. Our ship, The President Wilson, weighed anchor at 4 p.m., Oct. 14, and headed for Japan with a brief stopover in Honolulu before arriving in Yokohama on Oct. 27.

During the past weeks, Psalm 37 had spoken to our hearts: "<u>Trust</u> in the Lord…<u>Delight</u> in the Lord…<u>Commit</u> thy way unto the Lord…<u>Rest</u> in the Lord." Almost daily since the 13th of September, we had to go back to these verses. Little did we realize the encouragement we would have on the day we were to board the President Wilson. As Bernie's brother, Clarence, was driving us to the ship, Bernie opened a letter from a sailor we had met in a meeting sometime back, and out fell a check for a large sum of money. It was his entire mustering out pay! Clarence had just been talking with us about wishing we were with a denominational mission that would supply all our support. I was able to show him the check and say, "Does the Lord supply our needs?" Another miracle!

OUR THIRD TERM IN JAPAN 1963 ~ 1968

Our Return trip

Our trip to Japan held some adventures for us. The ship stopped in Honolulu. We rented a Jeep and spent the day touring the city and surroundings, but were surprised when we boarded the ship in the evening to hear the announcement that the ship was leaving immediately! A tidal wave was coming in and he wanted to ride it out at sea rather than in the harbor. When the ship got out of the harbor, we waited as launches brought the passengers, including the captain, to the ship. While at sea, we also witnessed the transfer of a seaman from a freighter to our ship where there was a doctor to tend to his needs. After 75,000 miles of travel, we were back in Japan. Although it was raining terribly hard when our ship docked in Yokohama, how our hearts beat when

Ministry in Japan

we looked at the pier and saw Japanese believers and several missionaries standing under umbrellas waving us a "Welcome home!" Later as we stood in the pulpit of Morning Glory Church and saw the familiar faces as well as new ones, we could not help but thank the Lord for His keeping power. What a joy it was to be back in the homes again for times of fellowship.

Radio

We praised God for the recent developments in radio and TV. It was 1964 and we were airing the Gospel on 94 of Japan's 120 commercial stations. We started a series of four weekly telecasts on a network of 28 stations. This in spite of the indirect opposition of Soka Gakkai. What an opportunity for sowing the Seed!

Korea Trip - Bernie

I was urged again by TEAM Korea's radio station in Inchon (near Seoul) to help out on a temporary basis. The situation was desperate. There were only seven people trying to run a 50,000 watt station twelve hours a day broadcasting the Gospel in four different languages: Korean, Chinese, Russian, and English. The need was for me to train programming staff. This would be a tremendous task for which God's guidance and strength would be needed. Being apart would be hard on our family, but this was what we believed the Lord would have us do.

HLKX is located on the salt beds outside the city of Inchon, 35 miles south of the Demilitarized Zone that divides North from South Korea. There is an unobstructed line of transmission across the Yellow Sea to Red China. We already had several letters from Manchuria and Russia. Because of a large number of American armed forces stationed near the transmitter, there was an excellent opportunity to present the Gospel to them as well. One hundred and one hours a week the Gospel was proclaimed in four languages on the standard broadcast band to those behind the iron and bamboo curtains.

Whenever I am away, Jeanette thinks up some project to do! This time she arranged to have a new ceiling put in the whole downstairs. The previous ceiling was just boards laying loose on a frame. Dust was always coming down and the heat was escaping. It was a big project, but improved our home immensely.

Back in Japan

We were encouraged when we received a letter from a Japanese lady living in Shanghai, China, who was saved while listening to one of PBA"s programs broadcast from Okinawa. Her brother, who lived in Tokyo, passed the letter on to us.

We rejoiced the way the Lord answered prayer for PBA's 1966 Easter rally, held annually on the roof of a large department store in the open air. Good weather was imperative. We were a little fearful to waken and find a cold, rainy day, but the Lord spoke peace to our hearts, and by noon there was a complete change.

We reveled in the warm physical sunshine as well as the consciousness of God's love. Around 2000 were in attendance at that rally! Over 200 decision cards were turned in by the unsaved. This does not mean that all these were saved, but it does show an interest. We were encouraged at the dedication and open house for our new office building. Jeanette had prepared sandwiches and cool drinks for all who attended.

For several years, the Lord had impressed PBA with the need for a daily radio program that would become nationwide. In 1967, a large grant from Tyndale House Publishers convinced us this was God's time to step out in faith. The grant also encouraged missions and missionaries to trust the Lord and launch out with us. The result? On May first, we began broadcasting daily in ten areas which gave us approximately 65% of the total population as our potential audience. The response was two to four times greater than our weekly programs. We believed our next step should be five more areas by October and the remaining fifteen areas for complete nationwide coverage by the end of 1968. However, we would need consistent help from many sources.

I worked late hours preparing for a meeting which had to do with the five year plan of operation for PBA. God had blessed, and this ministry had grown steadily. Jeanette commented, "Really, as close as I am to PBA, I am amazed at all the various departments, and details which are a part of reaching this nation with radio and TV, so I think it is difficult for others to imagine all that is involved." We were expecting 2000 to attend our annual Christmas rally and praying many would be reached for Christ.

The Church

It was 1964, but in Japan it was Showa 39, the year of the Dragon. Another reminder that this country does not acknowledge the birth of Jesus even if they have Christmas celebrations. We must not forget the task is yet undone!

Brother Junji Hatori had been a blessing to the church for the past six years and it had grown. He believed the Lord was leading him to another ministry. Following his resignation, there was disagreement about the calling of a replacement. One of the most discouraging factors we faced in this land was the lack of godly pastors to take over the work of missionaries. We were thankful for Brother Iide who became our new pastor. Interestingly, near the end of WWII, Brother Iide was in training to become a Kamikaze pilot, but the war ended before he finished.

Ladies' Meeting - Jeanette

There were signs of encouragement in our church as well as in the ladies group. One of our ladies had been witnessing to a

Ministry in Japan

neighbor and brought her to a meeting. The lady wept through almost the whole service while I was speaking. She said that Soka Gakkai had been after her day and night, but she did not believe that was her heart's need. "But today, I know I have found the answer, and I want to be saved." When she returned home, the neighbor ladies went with her and led her husband to the Lord as well. They were both at church and testified of their new found faith in Christ the following Sunday. At the next midweek service, Mr. Koike said that he hadn't smoked all week and had saved the money he would have spent and wondered if he could give it to the church!

Thirty-five ladies plus 10 children crowded into our house for our Christmas meeting. After I had served the dinner and home baked goodies, I looked around at the faces of each and praised the Lord for the miracle that had brought them to salvation. There were perhaps only three or four who were not Christians: one a widow lady who said she deeply longed to know our Savior, but didn't know how she could bear the shame of being an unfaithful wife by deserting the care of her husband's god shelf which is her duty to carry on. After the ladies meeting, Mrs.

Chapter 3

Iida, who was saved along with her husband in our home in February (her husband died of cancer the end of October) said, "I cannot explain how much being in your home today has meant to me." In fact, all the ladies seemed reluctant to go – and they stayed until 4:30. That night when we crawled numbly into our bed, we wondered if it was worth all the time and expense for such doings, when both seem to be at such a premium but then we realized what the Lord had accomplished and knew we were on the right track.

We had an unusual experience in 1967. For the first time, a pastor of one of our supporting churches visited us on the field. It was Bro. Joe West, of Blessed Hope Baptist Church, of San Antonio, TX. We had the privilege of introducing him to each of those for whom he and his church had prayed. He spoke through an interpreter and some people were saved.

As the Pastor Iide of Morning Glory Church handed a gift to us at the Christmas party, we were humbled to hear him say, "We know you are lonesome for your children in America, but look at the audience and see how many children you have in Japan!" Our church was growing, and we feared that some did not come back from Sunday to Sunday because of the crowded conditions. There were usually 225 in a space designed for 150. Sunday school children had to leave before church as they could not be accommodated.

Skate Camp

Skate Camp was held at Matsubarako and after sitting, eating, sleeping on the floor, no bath for five days, and rice, and miso (fermented bean soup) for breakfast it was good to get home from the skate camp! Bernie loves miso soup and Jeanette doesn't mind it either – except for breakfast! We brought back memories of one of the most blessed times of our whole stay in Japan as we watched 20 of the high school and university students get saved or firmly established in Christ and His Word. Miss Osumi was one of those. She made a profession the night Bro. Joe West, of San Antonio, TX, spoke in our church.

While at camp, she was just bubbling over as she received the assurance of her salvation and learned something of what it meant to be a Christian. The next Sunday at church, she came to us moaning, "Oh it's terrible, it's terrible to think I got in on the blessing of that camp and yet so many didn't." Then, as if we were to blame, she said, "Now why didn't more people come from Tokyo?" We reminded her we had invited all in the English class to come, but could get no response, and that she herself had been hesitant. She said, "Yes, you're right, but still it seems wasteful when so few came." To our sorrow, one young man named Shogo went away unsaved. He wasn't belligerent, but at testimony time said, "My heart has a piece of steel in it." What a thrill to hear the young man sitting next to him, who had just been saved at camp say, "Shogo, we are going to pray for you, and I hope our testimony as Christians will be hot enough to melt that steel."

The Olympics - Bernie

The Olympics were held in Tokyo in October, 1964. What a busy city! It seemed like every nerve and muscle was being strained in the great building program and preparation for that day. There were many evangelistic efforts to parallel the Olympics during the months of september and October.

The great XVIII Olympiad is now history, and we have to admit it was rather exciting living in this city where athletes from 94 countries participated in the games. Our thoughts were turned to a different kind of race and to another DAY when many athletes (Christians) who have won the prize will lay their medals (Crowns) at the feet of Jesus.

It was one of the busiest times of our lives without doubt. There were nights when we crawled into bed numb with tiredness, but we felt that every means possible should be employed to bring about a harvest of souls for Christ (out of every kindred, tongue, people, and nation.) Millions of tracts in several different languages were printed and distributed. Special meetings were held all over Japan, but particularly in Tokyo where there were three large meetings. The first was the early part of September. Over 18,000 were in attendance. The impression that lingers with us was the deep conviction that gripped the audience. People were weeping because of their sins. One meeting drew special attention. A Chinese evangelist spoke through an interpreter and I had charge of the music as well as directing the program. Two choirs from Korea participated, and some Christian athletes gave their testimony. The Devil fought these meetings from beginning to end.

Our Young Ones - Jeanette

The years had passed too quickly in many ways and our children were now young adults. At times we felt a bit sorry to see them facing many of the pressures which we face. But we realize this is good training. We thanked the Lord that they are concerned about doing His will and not just their own personal pleasure. Paul had met a university student on the train, given him a tract, and invited him to church. He was there the next Sunday and continued to come. He was saved a couple weeks later and shortly afterwards his married sister came to church with him. Paul also kept himself busy working at PBA and helped lay a cement walk in front of our house.

Chapter 3

We praise the Lord that our two children were real missionaries in Japan. They spent a week together helping out at a Japanese Bible camp. Karen tried to find a job to earn some money to help with her college education. School work must go on, but Paul's advise is not to get involved with pole vaulting as he did and broke his arm! Karen did bookkeeping at PBA. Our treasurer, who had been bedridden for six months, finally had to fly back to the States for surgery.

Our family had lots of fun times together. Every Saturday, weather permitting; we rode our bikes five miles on a nice road to what was then called Roosevelt Park. Of course I packed a good lunch to eat at the park.

Another fun incident: one night I had just settled down on the sofa for what I thought would be a quiet time and began to read

the "Nihon Times". About that time, Bernie threw a dishcloth from the kitchen, and hit the newspaper. I was so exasperated I crushed the newspaper into a ball, and threw it on the floor! Karen and Paul, who were looking on, just roared! They were still laughing when Bernie came over and kissed me and apologized. Paul and Karen had been singing trios and duets with Bernie which had been fun for all of us. Karen had even accompanied Bernie when he sang.

Karen graduated in May, 1965 and believed the Lord was leading her into nursing which she planed to use on the mission field. She left Japan on Sept. 2, and went to the Jim Bell family in Portland, OR. Jim was a Navy friend of ours whose daughter, Ginny Sue, a former playmate of Karen's, was going to nursing school with her. Karen would have a full schedule for the next three years with very little vacation. She had 26 hours of classes the first year. There were many adjustments to make in a "foreign land." The first year was very expensive, but she received a $300 scholarship. Along with other gifts, that provided for at least half of her needs for the school year. We were very touched by the kindness of a Japanese teenage girl who gave Karen a gift of $5. She said she wanted to give what she had saved to Karen because she was leaving her home to prepare for the Lord's work. We rejoiced in the many ways the Lord provided for Karen. There was an empty spot in our home and hearts, but we could say we had real peace and even joy, for we knew she was in the will of the Lord.

One Sunday, we were thrilled by the decision of a young engineering student. He and two others came to our house a year ago asking us to teach them English, and we were sorry we had to turn them away, but we felt we already had more than we could handle. Paul later met this fellow on the street and invited him to come to church with us on the next Sunday. He came and stayed two hours after the service to talk with Bernie. His questions, one after another, proved how much thinking he had done. Before Bernie left, he accepted the Lord. He was baptized on December 26th.

Paul was out of school for the summer. What a joy it was for Bernie to have him at work with him each day. I packed three times as many sandwiches as I did for just Bernie! Karen was doing well and reported that she had been making A's in her studies in the hospital. She felt this was an answer to prayer as she had asked the Lord that she would become a good nurse. She was thrilled when she had a Japanese patient, a sailor in for emergency treatment, who didn't know a word of English.

They called Karen as they knew she could speak Japanese. Because of an inheritance which I had recently received, Karen was able to spend one month vacation with us during the summer. Paul would be leaving next summer and it would be two years before our family could be together again.

Ministry in Japan

In August, we had a gathering in our front yard, an occasion of much rejoicing, for it was Karen's homecoming! There were 20 in attendance. It was also the day of Mr. Shioda's conversion. Paul had met Mr. Shioda one day as he was walking our dog, Teddy, and his rubber ball went into Mr. Shioda's yard, and they had became good friends.

Paul graduated from high school, June 16. Karen entered another phase of her training – a three month course taking care of psychiatric patients in Salem, OR. We were thankful that, except for my fever a couple of years ago, we were very well this term.

Fall is the time when the leaves begin to change color, the weather is changing, mothers are putting summer clothes away, and the children start back to school. It was certainly true in the Holritz household, this fall even a bit more than usual. This year, the last of our chicks "flew the coop!" On September first, Paul boarded the plane for the U.S. to be met by his sister, Karen. After a time at a Labor Day Bible camp, he started classes at Multnomah School of the Bible, in Portland, OR.

For Karen there were changes as well. She returned to Portland after completing three months of difficult training at the Oregon State Mental Hospital, in Salem. Just as she finished this session, the school gave notice of a very delightful change in schedule. Hers would be the first class to graduate in mid-June instead of mid-September. This would be a very hard year with many difficult examinations. She was also a part of The Nurses' Christian Fellowship, a Bible witness to fellow students and patients alike.

Medical and Spiritual Miracle – The Koikes

Our ministry was full and varied, but the greatest joy was dealing personally with the lost, or with new born babes as Mrs. Koike

and her husband pictured in the jacket. This was the couple who were so wondrously saved in 1964. Since that time, the Lord had given us a number of opportunities for fellowshipping and counseling. Mrs. Koike had a very serious heart condition, and needed an operation as soon as possible to replace a valve in the heart. This type of surgery had not been successful in Japan, so they feared for her life if she should have it done in this country

Terrific pressures were being brought upon this dear couple by Mrs. Koike's mother who claimed the "ill luck" was brought upon them because of their conversion from Buddhism to Christianity. She didn't seem to remember that her daughter was sickly before her conversion. They were further ridiculed when they had to call upon this grandmother to care for their little son while Mrs. Koike was in the hospital. Now they were faced with another problem. The house in which they live had been financed almost entirely by Mrs. Koike's parents who were strong Buddhist. The family god shelf was stored in their home. Since their conversion, they had kept its doors closed and refused to make the daily offerings. Now the parents were after them to take the god shelf out of the house which meant they could ask them to leave, and the god shelf remain instead. This would be a real hardship, especially in view of Mrs. Koike's health. We prayed much for this spiritual battle.

The early part of March, 1965, we sent a special letter asking prayer for Mr. & Mrs. Koike. This letter reached some very dear friends in St. Paul, Bill and Evelyn Kredit, whom we had known from our Navy days. They passed it on to Evelyn's brother-in-law, Herb McDonald. Herb had contact with a Mrs. Ramsey, who sponsored patients with dire medical needs to come to America for treatment. She agreed to bring both Mr. and Mrs. Koike to the States so that she might have the critical surgery. All expenses paid!

Her surgery to replace the mitral valve went well, but for several days she laid in a coma. Our dear friends in Minneapolis had been notified that, unless a miracle took place, she would not recover from her deathlike sleep. But God in His mercy awakened her on a Sunday night, and by Tuesday all concerned felt she had made it over the hump! A week later she was back in her own hospital room, smiling and reading her Bible. Truly "the God of all flesh" had answered prayers, and filled our hearts with joy and thanksgiving. John 16:24. After six long months in America, our dear Mrs. Koike returned to Japan, thankful for all that God had done for her. She was in excellent shape, but had to remain careful for several years.

Chapter 3

We were so thankful for the many Christian friends who visited her regularly and helped through various trials and suffering. Everyone who had written told us of the blessing of visiting Mrs. Koike was to visit in spite of the language barrier. She was speaking English fairly well by the time she left the U.S. Through her faithful testimony, she was able to lead her roommate, a twenty year old girl from Greece, to the Lord. They read the Bible everyday, each in her own language.

We continued to pray for Mrs. Koike's parents. They promised to believe in her God if she made it safely back from this operation. Her mother had also promised to take care of her daughter during her long convalescence, but refused to do either. We would have to see how our God would work this one out. The verse that Mrs. Koike said was on her heart since returning was "To whom much is given; much is required." Luke 12:48

Ministry in Japan

Mrs. Mori

Only eternity will tell how many have been influenced by the dedicated lives of the Iwasaki family. One was Mrs. Mori, who had grown up with Mrs. Iwasaki as a child. They had lost contact with each other during the war until one day, Mrs. Iwasaki got a telephone call from a mutual friend, and thus they met again after sixteen years. Mrs. Mori realized that this was not the same friend that she had known before. There was something different and she was much impressed. One day when she was visiting our home, Paul looked up at her and said, "I'm praying for you, Mrs. Mori." She seemed delighted. Three years later, Mrs. Mori, well known for her flower arranging and has her own TV program, discovered, in spite of her success, the emptiness of her own life, and was gloriously saved. She never travels without tracts and has given all her students a New Testament.

Every Christmas, we get together with the Iwasaki family for a meal. This time, Mrs. Mori asked if she and her two sons could join us. She wanted her boys to see what Christmas was like in a Christian home and especially to see how our families were knit

together as one. (Pictured left to right - Mrs. Iwasaki, Mrs. Mori, her son, Iwasaki's son, Paul, Iwasaki's son, Mrs. Mori's son, Mr.

Iwasaki's brother. Sorry Mr. Iwasaki and daughter, Bernie and Jeanette did not get in the, picture.)

We had a rather unusual evening one night in 1967 – we don't often get invited to the Hilton Hotel for dinner! The party was a wedding dinner for Mrs. Mori's youngest son now returned from America. At the time, Mrs. Mori's husband was not a Christian and of the fifty or so guests, including a member of the Japanese Parliament, there was only a handful of Christians. Mrs. Mori was given permission to make the arrangements for the program and she was most anxious that a testimony for her Savior be given. So she asked Mr. Iwasaki to be the emcee and Bernie to sing, "Jesus is All the World to Me." Mrs. Mori had a testimony before many Americans as well as Japanese. As is often the case, her flower arrangements were being displayed in leading department stores.

The neighborhood

In addition to an already busy schedule, one of the most interesting aspects is what a missionary will be called on to do next. One day Mrs. Hara, a little old grandmother across the street phoned Jeanette and asked, "Won't you please come and sit with me until this terrible thunderstorm is over. I'm so afraid." Jeanette left her supper preparations in order to be of service in this small way. Whenever Mrs. Hara would start her kerosene heater it would make a small "pop" so she would call Jeanette if her family wasn't around. On another day Bernie was asked to carry an electric blanket to a man in a TB sanitarium. He was thankful for this opportunity as he had been witnessing to this man ever since we had come to Japan.

Living near us was a man and his family who was a true servant of the Lord. Mr. Eiyama had been led to Christ by a missionary and wanted to do anything he could to help them. On One occasion we needed to build a shed in our backyard. Mr. Eiyanna came early each morning before he went to work until it was done.

We felt this was another reason we were so glad our mission wanted us to live among the nationals.

DID YOU KNOW?
Japan has a modern crack train such as this now the fastest in the world? Japan can also boast of the tallest tower, new super highways, huge department stores with escalators, and most of the

Chapter 3

homes have television sets. (Of course, since most of this had sprung up in the past few years, Japan still has some of its old and not so modern ways.)

DID YOU KNOW?
That the people of Japan are the most educated in the world and 99% of them can read?

DID YOU KINOW?
That in spite of all the education and modern ways, Japan still has as many gods as people, plus thousands of heathen temples and superstitions that blind and bind, and make it very difficult for them to become Christians? In fact, we are almost sure there is not a country in the world that is anymore in bondage to idols and superstitions than Japan. One day in a Tokyo English newspaper, there was a picture of a service being held at one of these modern department stores in honor of the spirits of the broken Sheaffer fountain pens!

Boys' Day

Ministry in Japan

On Boys' Day a pole is place in the family's yard with a flying carp, one for each boy. The carp represents the spirit of a boy. As a carp is strong swimming against the stream, courageous and adventuresome, he is the epitome of a boy. Then there are dolls of Samurai soldiers and Sumo wrestlers taken out and displayed in the house. The boys dress up and play with wooden swords. There is a visit to the local Shinto shrine.

Girls' Day

On Girls' Day there is a special display of dolls that represent the imperial court. The girls dress in elaborate kimonos and go out doors and play a badminton type of game. The paddles are flat

wood, and the shuttle is a hard bean like object with feathers on it. Sometime during the day they visit the local Shinto shrine. One day the people across the street from us dressed Karen up in one of those kimonos and took a picture of her in front of the doll display in their house.

Furlough preparations

Our return to the States this time was different as we were asked to remain for a three year trial period as the U.S. Representative for PBA. At the end of the three year trial the situation would be reviewed by TEAM, PBA, and ourselves as to whether we remained in the States as the representative or return to Japan. Everyone felt that for the sake of PBA, we should settle in Wheaton, IL near our mission headquarters.

Because of the nature of our new assignment, preparations for departure were the most difficult of our lives. Except for our suitcases which were to be carried with us on the plane, everything was being sorted into one of seven piles: sell, store, loan, ship ahead, carry with us, give away, or toss. Every time we went through this process we decided a missionary shouldn't own anything. Then somehow we'd forget and started collecting. After all is said and done, we enjoyed all that the Lord gave us while we had it. Our house, called by one Japanese brother one of the most impossible he had ever seen, was transformed by a little paint, curtains, etc, into a comfortable little haven for us and those who had visited within its walls. On May 29, 1968, we flew back to the USA. It was rather difficult to describe our feelings: the joy of rejoining our children again after almost three years of separation, (except for one month when Karen came back to Japan) and yet the pain of leaving those who had become, through Christ, so precious to us.

Before leaving Japan I took part with the Japan TEAM missionaries in making a record to be sold in the States. Copies of the accompaniment of my solos were used as I sang in my meetings. The proceeds from the sale of the records were used to buy a piano for the mission center in Tokyo.

Chapter Four
Our Ministry in the US: 1968~1992

PBA JAPAN'S REPRESEENTATIVE IN THE U. S. 1968 ~ 1981

In the States – 1968 - Bernie

We arrived in the States in time to witness Karen's graduation from nursing school. What a joy it was to have our family together again. It was a reminder of the joy there will be in the mansions above when all the family of those who have put their trust in the Savior will be together forever to behold His lovely face. The Lord answered above our expectation and provided a nice little house in a quiet neighborhood in Portland for only ninety-five dollars a month! As we reviewed the circumstances that led to the renting of this place, it was evident that the Lord was saving it just for us. The same was true of our Dodge Coronet which had been used as a Driver's Education car and we were able to purchase reasonably through a Christian dealer. We were thankful for a car that would be adequate for the thousands of miles we would travel. All we had to do was to get used to the fantastic speed and driving on the "wrong side" of the road!

We praised the Lord for delivering us from a mishap that could have been tragic. I had been waiting in our car in the parking lot while Jeanette was shopping, but suddenly felt I should join her in the grocery store. While I was absent, a man trying to park his car pushed his accelerator to the floor instead of the brake pedal and crashed into the rear of our car ramming it into the car in

Ministry in the U.S.

front of us sending it into a car twenty feet away! Our car was repaired – easier than I would have been! A miracle of God's protection.

When Karen and Paul heard that we were assigned to the States, they wanted to know where we were going to settle. They were delighted to learn that we were thinking of Wheaton, IL, because they wanted to enroll in Moody Bible Institute to prepare for missionary service. We were thankful that though they would be living in the dormitory, they would be near enough to visit on weekends when we were not on the road.

As the four of us left Portland with Akio Iwasaki, on his way to enroll in the Bible Institute of Los Angeles (BIOLA), we were startled by a roaring forest fire. We did not know that in a few more days we would not only see two more but be caught between them! How wonderful to be delivered out of the fire.

Chapter 4

After spending a few days with Max and Estelle Hayes, we left Akio with them to take to Los Angeles, and started on our way to Chicago, camping in our tent every night. Knowing that our journey across the country would occupy many hours, we asked the Lord to speak to our hearts and He did. The book of Acts was our text, and the theme was "The Way of Faith." How precious the lessons. When we arrived in Wheaton, we were thankful for the furnished apartment at our TEAM Headquarters. Paul and Karen settled into the dorms at Moody Bible Institute.

Radio

Word from Japan informed us that Satan's challenge to our advance seemed to be in three areas: 1) opposition from the main station in Tokyo, which caused us to change stations, 2) loss of personnel due to marriages, and furloughs, 3) shortage of funds because of the need during August to subsidize by more than $5,000 the mission sponsoring the daily program. It was very apparent that there was much need for deputation work in behalf of the radio ministry in Japan. By the end of October, we were forced to drop the nine stations carrying our daily broadcast because of lack of support. Another challenge was Art Seely, the general manager of PBA, had been ordered to rest for two or three months because of exhaustion and there was no one to take his place!

In a recent trip south, I spoke 46 times in 49 days. Jeanette was able to see several members of her family and rejoiced to see the Lord at work among them. We found out that we were not as young as we used to be, but after getting some rest, we were ready to go again.

In early 1969, our meetings took us as far east as Washington, DC, south to the Carolinas, and northwest as far as Minnesota. Other than that, most of our meetings were nearby: Illinois, Indiana, and Michigan. But our longest trip was in October as we journeyed to Oregon for our mission's annual conference, as well as two other conferences in Washington.

During the past year, we have sensed the Lord's guidance in our new assignment as the North American Representative for PBA. A board of references and advisors was set up; giving had increased; and publication problems were worked out. Dr. Hatori,

our radio pastor from Japan, and I took a five week tour. There was a challenge in television evangelism which they wanted to share with the churches of America. The meetings started in Florida, continued up the east coast as far as New Jersey, then across the north to Chicago, ending October 26th.

As the PBA representatives, we realized how hard it is to feel a part of the team when you are so far from where the action is. Yet this is where the Lord had placed us for the present. A letter from one of our missionaries said, "Never have the doors of Japan been more open to the Gospel." This made us anxious to utilize every opportunity to announce the "good tidings of great joy."

A new worker joined our ministry, Mrs. Del Langford from our supporting church in South Carolina. She said the Lord led her to quit her job in Greenville, in order to help us with this ministry. With the work piling up because of moving, we don't know what we would have done without her. She would need to find another job until we could raise enough to support her full time. Our concern was that she not overdo.

When we considered the budget for the new fiscal year which began April 1, 1970, we asked the Lord to give us an additional thousand dollars a month for the work. Art Seely's health improved, but Akira Hatori was indirectly involved in a car accident which trapped him for an hour in a tunnel! The strain was too much for his heart and he had to cancel all his appointments except his radio preaching for two months.

As we read testimonies of people like Mr. Tanaka, we realized the reality of Satan's power over the lives of Japan's millions. It stirred a sense of urgency within us. Mr. Tanaka, a follower of the militant religion, Soka Gakkai, became disturbed about the problem of death. He asked the people in Soka Gakkai for the answer, but instead they threatened him. His aged mother, who had contact with Christianity as a child, suggested he borrow a Bible from a Christian who lived nearby. He said, "Much of it was hard to understand until I came to the words, 'Come unto me all ye that labor and are heavy laden and I will give you rest,' and I knew these words were written for me. Then I heard your program, *The Light of the World*, and sent for the free correspondence Bible course which was offered. My fear of death was caused by sin in my heart, and you told me that Jesus died for all my sins, and I should ask Him to forgive me, and give me a new life. This I did, and can testify now that all is taken care of, and I have no more fear."

This was the first summer we spent time in Bible camps and it was very rewarding, especially the family camps. It was a wonderful time to present missions all week long to the same group. We were thankful for the interest shown in the ministry of PBA through these and many other contacts. (The July remittance was the largest ever.) It was suggested by the field that I visit Japan in 1971 to get a fresh view of what was going on, as well as gather material. The work had grown, and we were seeing the blessing of the Lord.

During 1971, a number of the PBA missionaries had serious illnesses, but had improved, and had returned to the field. The new radio program, *Young Life Club*, had received a good response from the three areas where it was aired. Judging from the ages of those who wrote us, we were right on target. There was a good Easter rally with 1500 in attendance. A hundred and forty came forward to accept Christ. These new converts were very much alone as far as encouragement was concerned.

In December of 1966, while we were still in Japan, the Iwasakis and Holritzes (Karen was already in the U.S.) were asked to ap-

pear on PBA's Christmas TV broadcast in Tokyo. Our two families have been very close and always shared our Christmases together. The idea was to show what Christ meant to each of us and how His love could bind the families of two nations as one. PBA received this surprising letter... "On Christmas eve five years ago, I was watching a TV Christmas program. Two families, Japanese, and American, were talking together. I felt something touched my heart strings when I saw the joyful faces of both families. I was strongly impressed at that time, I think because I realized I lacked that kind of joy in my own life. I learned about PBA's Bible correspondence course through that program. As I continued to study the correspondence course, I came to understand that Jesus Christ died on the cross for me, and rose again after three days. I was completely changed, joy entered my life, and now I can be thankful even for difficulties that come."

Praise the Lord for this testimony -- a reminder to keep sowing the seed.

Just a word about "Mom and Dad" Holritz; in 1972, we were busier than ever in meetings and office work. There was a definite need for office personnel. Mrs. Langford still gave her evenings for secretarial work, but we wanted to have her full time.

From the middle of January, the tempo in missionary conferences began to increase and we were involved in a number. As a result of these meetings, new support came in for PBA. We received a letter from a regular supporter of PBA increasing their giving as of January. All of this made it possible for us to get the Gospel to more Japanese. Praise the Lord!

We went through some deep waters in the fall when giving to PBA took a "nose dive." This caused much heart searching on our part, but the Lord showed us that the work we were doing here makes it possible for more Japanese to hear the Gospel of salvation. We dared not stop even though the going got tough at times.

During a visit from Dr. Hatori, we had five full days in meetings and conferences which clarified our vision, and new goals were established. On October 16, I left for Tokyo for three weeks with every minute packed! Jeanette had her hands full while he was gone. It was a blessing to meet Paul in Japan and have the joy of working with him as a fellow missionary on the field. He had already mapped out some things I had to do. His term of one year would be over at that time so we to returned to the States together.

Family

It was 1968, and Karen rejoiced in the privilege of studying the Bible all day long. She was enjoying taking lessons on the pipe organ, as well as her work in extension with young people. She was also one of the part-time nurses at Moody. Paul was in his second year of Bible school, majoring in Christian Education and Music. He was a member of the Moody Chorale which necessitated some travel. He was thrilled to lead several children to the Lord in his extension work.

In 1969, we were asked to move from our reasonably priced apartment at our mission to make room for another missionary family returning from the field, and to find housing within our budget for ourselves, and for the PBA office that keeps expanding. Rent was fantastically high and our time for house hunting was limited, but we knew the Lord would provide.

This was to an unfurnished house which we bought. An inheritance from Jeanette's grandmother made it possible for us to pay down on the house and the interest rate for the mortgage was four and a quarter percent! You can imagine what this was like since all we owned was clothes, dishes, and books. Though unsettled, we had a number of Japanese visitors from overseas.

We had almost furnished our house, but weren't as fortunate as we were last furlough when friends helped us to find the things we needed. We picked up some good bargains at damaged freight, but it was time consuming. Margaret Nendick, a sweet

Chapter 4

Christian neighbor lady, took Jeanette on "garage sale trips" while I was away in meetings or too busy to take her.

Jeanette

We enjoyed having Paul home for a few days after his semester exams. Can you imagine what it would be like for a mother to live alone with two men, her husband and son, who love to tease? They asked me why I hadn't made a particular dish that they liked and I said, "You hadn't commented on it so I threw the recipe away!" After that they commented on everything! "This is such good peanut butter; this is such good salt and pepper; this is such good butter;" for fear I might take them off the table! When Karen came home, the three of them got in a couple of good sessions of ice skating. I did not have the nerve to try! I stayed in most of the time, as I was not used to this cold weather which got down to 16 below one night! I'm still a Texan! It was nice for me to have Karen living at home as she kept me company in the evenings while Bernie was in Oregon and Washington.

Five days after school was out in 1970, Paul left for Word of Life Bible Camp in New York where he would be for the summer. He received valuable training and experience which would not only prepare him for his work as a dorm counselor at Moody in the fall, but also for whatever the Lord had for him in the future. Karen passed her nursing validation for the University of Illinois Medical College, and she only needed a year and a half to receive her BSN. She started working at a local hospital to meet expenses for the next school year. She and I taught at our home church's VBS while Bernie was away in meetings.)

Bernie kept me busy writing all our personal correspondence. In addition to housework, I had developed a "green thumb." We had a garden plot in our backyard which gave me time outside and also helped with our food budget.

Each of our family had contact with Japanese in this country. We met a young Japanese doctor and his wife in a nearby park. His schedule was heavy, but we were eventually able to arrange a time for them to be with us for church and Sunday dinner. It was the first time they had ever been in a church and, though they didn't understand much, they seemed to enjoy it. A few weeks later they dropped by to see us again and brought with them another Japanese doctor who had just arrived in America. We were encouraged and anxious to win those two couples to Christ.

At last a family picture! During 1971, after a number of attempts in our own home to make a family photo and other complications too numerous to mention, we finally had it done professionally. We trust it will be a reminder of the faithfulness of the Lord in answer to prayers through the years.

Chapter 4

The Lord says that we should give thanks. WE PRAISE HIM FOR:
> Allowing us these many years of ministry to the Japanese.

> Bernie's fruitful and safe journey to Japan in Feb. & March.

> The Lord wonderfully provided everything.

Daily financial needs supplied. There have been crises, but we always came out the better when we found how dependent we were upon Him and rejoiced all the more when we saw His answers!

Paul graduated from the University of Illinois in June, 1971, and went to Word of Life in New York, this time as a leader of counselors. He applied to Tennessee Temple University for the fall

Ministry in the U.S.

semester, but received an invitation to work with PBA in Tokyo for a year. Karen was thankful for the many who were interceding for her. She did well in her studies at the University of Illinois, and was installed into the National Honor Society of Nurses (comparable to Phi Beta Kai.) She decided to go as a counselor to Word of Life for the summer.

The most thrilling event of 1972 was the way in which the Lord provided for Paul and sent him to Japan with only one week's delay in his scheduled departure. This was especially amazing since he was at Word of Life Camp after graduation from Moody until September 8th, which left very little time for deputation, packing, etc. But, in those few short weeks, he received the necessary funds for travel as well as monthly support! Paul wrote from Japan that he was absolutely amazed at all the opportunities for service. In addition to work at PBA, he helped in an English Bible camp, MK meetings, played piano solos at two rallies, and called on a number of contacts who were in need of salvation.

Twenty-two years ago we sailed from Portland, OR, for Japan to begin our missionary work. What wonderful miracles God had done to make that possible. As we look back, we see it was a long series of blessings in which many people played a major role. We thank God for each of them.

Another bit of exciting news was Karen's choice of a field of service. The indications were that the Lord wanted her in Rhodesia and she was making preparations in that direction. In the interim, she taught nursing at the University of Illinois which was valuable training as she would serve in the same capacity in TEAM's hospital in Rhodesia. Since Karen had lived with us the past two years, she would be starting "from scratch" as far as outfit was concerned. From all the activity around this house you would think that we were all going to Rhodesia. It was a family project. What a thrill to see the Lord move in her behalf in so many ways. The date of departure was set – the end of

January, 1973. There were still support and outfit needs, but it was taking shape.

Church in Japan

November 1970, marked the twentieth anniversary of Morning Glory Church. They had special evangelistic meetings to reach new people; then a few days for a spiritual retreat for the membership. The Lord had blessed the work. Many who started in Sunday school have become leaders in the church. One of the members was already on the mission field, and a couple left for South America in October.

Friends in Japan

During our early days in Japan – over twenty years ago -- we began witnessing to Mike Ikehata. His response was, "I feel sorry for you, Mr. Holritz, you need someone to help you. I can take care of myself." Since we returned to the States, Phil Foxwell had continued calling on Mike in the TB sanitarium. While he

appreciated these visits and often said a few foreigners were the only friends that he had left, still he would not come to the Savior. Previous to Bernie's trip to Japan in February, 1971, we had no new word concerning Mike. Imagine Bernie's joy when he spotted Mike in a service where he was preaching shortly after his arrival in Tokyo. It was good to learn that Mike would soon be released from the TB sanitarium. But better yet, was to hear from his own lips that he had confessed Christ as Savior last fall! There were numerous complications to unravel -- No one wanted to hire a 51 year old man who had been in a TB sanitarium for five years.

PBA Japan's Representative in U.S. FROM 1973 ~ 1977

Radio - Bernie

Jeanette and I prepared for meetings in Indiana, Illinois, and Michigan in March, and a trip south in April, 1973. We had a wonderful trip in deputation for PBA that was six weeks in duration with meetings and travel every day. There was new support raised as well as increase from those who already supported PBA. This would help with the devaluation of the dollar in Japan. After we returned home, we took part in several mission conferences and scratched to dig ourselves out of the stack of work that piled up during our absence. The summer months were very full. July first, Art Seely and Dr Hatori were with us. Some major plans and decisions were made and the stateside board met for the first time. During the first half of August, the pastor of our church in Tokyo and the head deacon visited us.

This was one of the most eventful years of our home assignment. I was amazed at the way the Lord had opened up so many meetings. I had 49 meetings and conferences in fifteen states and was booked as full as I dared through July, 1974. The mailing list had grown and so had the list of donors. The average monthly donations represented about one third of the total Japan budget.

Chapter 4

A year ago, it was suggested by several of our advisors, that PBA seek stateside incorporation and IRA recognition. Both of these were completed during 1973. (After all that experience, I felt like I had graduated from law school and had passed the bar!) What would this mean? Instead of operating financially under the umbrella of three missions as heretofore, we would now handle the finances ourselves. Otherwise, there were no changes.

Another thrilling development had been a new slide/tape presentation for PBA. This was our son, Paul's; responsibility entirely. Since April, it had numerous showings. One mission incorporated it into their library and we have negotiated with other missions to do the same. Speaking of Paul, it was a delight to have him working as my office manager in addition to his schooling. This allowed me more time to contact individuals and churches. I was also very indebted to Mrs. Langford, my secretary, and besides her, two men who helped me with all the graphics. I can not forget the fantastic help Jeanette was to me.

As we heard almost daily of so many fields where there was much opposition to the Gospel and many being driven out or killed, we thank the Lord for the door that is so wide open in Japan which inspired us to push ahead with new projects in 1974.

We were booked all the way to the middle of July, 1974, with meetings in Nebraska, Colorado, New Mexico, Arizona, Missouri, Illinois, and Michigan. We were thankful for good health in order to carry this kind of a schedule. As a result of these meetings, at least two churches were considering support for PBA. In a meeting in Missouri, a Japanese lady trusted Christ as her Savior.

Our Plans for a Trip to Japan

Every two years, it was necessary for me to visit the field to coordinate the activities of the US office with PBA Japan, and renew my vision and burden, but this time I would not be going alone. As we prayed about the trip, we felt that it was time for Jeanette to go as well. She is a very important part of this work, and many of our Japanese friends had also asked her to come. We trusted the Lord to make this financially possible. Four shots were a painful reminder of a host of preparations necessary before we left for Japan. Jeanette's passport must be renewed; gifts purchased and carefully packed for those dear friends with whom we had such close fellowship during our years of ministry in Japan. Each day had to be carefully planned so as to make the best use of time.

After we arrived in Japan, while I was busy at the PBA office, Jeanette found out what it was like to walk again as she visited the homes of dear friends we led to the Lord many years ago. One such visit in Tokyo itself meant one and a half hours on the train and forty to fifty minutes walking, and that in pouring down rain, but she loved every minute of it. It was like old times as her dearest Japanese friend, Mrs. Iwasaki, and she had the opportunity to call on several unsaved friends, and urged them to come to Christ.

We also had a wonderful opportunity of meeting the Koike's, whom we led to the Lord in our third term on the field. (She was the one who had open heart surgery in the States.) Through the Koike's unusual testimony, many have come to the Savior, but Mrs. Koike's parents were still stubbornly resisting the Gospel. Mrs. Iwasaki and she called on them. They were convinced that, if ever they saw a case of demon possession, that was it. They spoke of all that their gods had done, even attributing their daughter's healing to Buddha, and mentioned how on occasion their god's of stone literally moved on their shelves, and uttered sounds! Our enemy, the Devil, had shown his strength in his dealings with Mrs. Koike's parents. If a person refuses to see the light when it is so evident, his heart becomes more hardened.

Chapter 4

June 30, marked the end of PBA's fiscal year. Preparations for our first audit reminded us of the Lord's goodness by the steady increase of support to PBA over the past six years.

Report on Trip to Japan – Bernie

The smothering pressing crowds, the noise, and the wild traffic of Tokyo had faded from our memories until it was quickly revived as we drove from the airport in the fast moving traffic with only inches between us and the cars before, behind, and on either side. At times we even thought they were above and below, but decided it must be our jumpy nerves playing tricks on us! In spite of the hustle and bustle, once again came the quiet and assuring conviction that Japan was the land of God's calling for us even though our ministry was that of supplying those on the "front lines." God blessed my messages to the staff of PBA at their annual retreat, and there seemed to be renewed vision to press ahead in the battle for souls so bound by the satanic darkness of that land.

Little did I realize that the day I was to visit my brother, Adolph, while en route to meetings in Canada would be the day of his funeral! Adolph died suddenly of an aneurism. Jeanette quickly packed and drove with me to Minnesota but returned home alone by plane. It was a strange feeling to be reading Adolph's recent letter with a map and directions as we drove to their new home in Lindstrom. I sang for the funeral and the Lord gave me strength to do so, as well as several opportunities to witness to relatives. Adolph was a Christian so that was very comforting.

As we entered 1975, we were thankful for the many doors opened to us, and the way the Lord had laid the burden of PBA on people's hearts both to give and to pray. During 1974, PBA faced one of its severest financial tests. As we prayed, the Lord gave assurance that He would answer. Although we were not

Ministry in the U.S.

"out of the woods," it was thrilling to see what the Lord was doing. Apparently He was preparing us for a greater work ahead.

Since my meetings in Canada, we were in Kentucky for a family camp where I was co-speaker with a dear black brother, Dr. William Banks, formerly a professor at Moody Bible Institute. The Lord touched our hearts with his humility and Spirit-filled ministry. When the camp was over, Dr. Banks invited me to come to his church in Philadelphia for a meeting.

It was 1976 and we were in the midst of preparation for PBA's twenty-fifth anniversary meetings. Dr. Hatori would be in the US in October so we had planned banquets in Los Angeles, San Jose, Spokane, Seattle, and Chicago with some side trips to other parts of the country. What a volume of correspondence was involved! We felt it was imperative to acquaint our brothers and sisters in Christ with this ministry. It had been a good year for PBA and we had experienced an abundant supply of every need. A very unexpected gift came which cleared up a deficit that had occurred in our TEAM account due to a continuing lack of support.

As Jeanette and I thought about the trip I was to make to Japan, it was almost overwhelming: so many things to prepare. The only dates that seemed to be open were Nov. 18 – Dec.8, 1977. My last stateside meeting was Nov. 16 and the next was Dec. 20. The folks in Japan did a great job in arranging my schedule, but could I get it all done? Looking back at the specific answers to prayer as well as the crucial visit to Japan, one verse describes what took place, "Exceeding abundantly above all that we ask or think."

Family

Ever since Paul came home in 1972, his training in College of DuPage enabled him to set up financial and office procedures as

Chapter 4

PBA was being incorporated and applying for IRS recognition. As the work progressed, he was able to train volunteers to handle certain areas of the work. Then our church called him to become their visitation pastor. This additional experience would be valuable as he continued to prepare for missionary service, but he would have to take some summer courses in order to graduate in August. Being Visitation Pastor and student at the same time was a heavy load!

Paul finished his courses at College of DuPage in the fall of 1973. Both he and Bernie were heavily engaged in PBA work. Jeanette was kept busy in the home, as well as serving as a deaconess at our church. The Lord gave us both health and strength for the work He called us to do.

The Hidden Diamond - Jeanette

What could be more precious than a diamond, especially when it had been put my finger 30 years ago by someone who loves me dearly. We had just come back from a week's vacation and I was anxious to get the laundry done. It was a beautiful day and the best time to hang clothes out of doors. In the midst of a perfectly peaceful day, I suddenly discovered, to my horror, that my diamond had fallen out of my ring. After that it was chaos! Bernie and Paul, who was living with us, first went out to search in the tall grass which had not been mowed since we left. Then they spent a fruitless two hours looking in the washing machine and drier and then the traps of the drains. I spent a long time at the sink bemoaning what had happened. I was even hoping the diamond would come out of the faucet!

After about a week, I had to deal with myself. I confessed to the Lord that if I ever got the diamond back, it would have to be His doing and not mine. A few days later, we went to see the *Passion Play* in Zion, IL. It got quite late and on the way home I fell asleep. When we arrived, I went directly to our bedroom and switched on the light. My eyes saw a bright glimmer from a spot in the heavy carpet. Trembling, I picked it up and went running out to Paul, who was in the living room and I said, "What is this?" He said, "Mom, it's your diamond. Haven't you been praying for it?" Diamond found! A miracle of God's grace. "Oh ye of little faith."

The Peeping Tom – Jeanette

One day we awoke to find a garbage can turned upside down in front of one our bedrooms. We were a bit puzzled until we realized this was our daughter's bedroom where a young lady had been staying and the garbage can would allow a person to be the right height so that whatever he was looking for would have been in full view!

We had almost forgotten this incident when one morning at about 3 a.m. I was in the bathroom doing some last minute clean-up before we were to leave for Japan and workaholic that I am, I wanted the house to be left in order before we left. Suddenly I saw a face in the window. I let out a low blood curdling scream and was thankful that Bernie heard me. Bernie quickly called the police and they said they had the same kind of reports from others in the neighborhood!

Another late night, the police came and said they had cornered a man in the parking lot of the church in the neighborhood. Since there was no one else to identify the likeness of this man, they would drive me to the parking lot and put the spotlight on him to see if I could recognize him. When I saw him, I gasped; it was he alright!

Then they asked to cross examine me in court which, of course, I did not want to do. I prayed long and hard to see if God would sympathize with my plight. "Forgive me, Father, for ever doubting you." The next day the court called and said, "George Fox had admitted his guilt and you do not have to appear." All it cost him was a hundred dollars and a chance to start over again, but thankfully not in our neighborhood.

Bernie's Surgery

Bernie had an appointment with the doctor the middle of December. We really didn't expect him to tell us that Bernie was to enter the hospital Jan 12, 1976, for surgery. However, there was a bladder infection which needed to be cleared up first. We had just competed plans for meetings in Texas! Those plans had to be canceled. There was a momentary shock from such news, but as we waited before the Lord, He gave peace, calm, and strength -- "The Lord directs our steps   and our stops."

Jeanette's Summer Project

Bernie was shocked when he returned from one of his trips to see a pile of clay clods at one end of my garden. A huge sycamore

tree in front of the garden area had tenaciously spread its roots into the garden as if it owned the place, stealing the nutrients, and turning my nice soil into hard clay! I thought I'd had enough of this, and proceeded to dig up the clay. I pitched it with my shovel to the garden's edge. Now what was I to do with the huge chasm, and no soil with which to fill it? In the meantime, our next door neighbors had ordered a truckload of beautiful black soil dumped in their yard to be used later to cover their lawn. I kept my eye on the soil thinking that was just what I needed. (Do you call that covetousness?) I never dreamed that the lady would say one day, "I'm so tired of looking at this soil, and I know that Bill is not going to do anything about it, so I'm going to call a truck to take it out of our yard." Then I meekly said, "May I have it?" She replied, "Yes, it would save me the price of having it taken out of here." Then I realized, if that soil were to get to my garden, it would have to be by wheelbarrow. But in time, my mission was accomplished! (A friend of Paul had a pickup truck and he hauled the clay clods away.)

Now I want to give you a different story about my garden, but I will have to do some explaining. At the back of our garden was a beautiful, but not very strong, basket weave fence. For some reason, the children in the homes behind us loved to climb on it. One day there were some children about to climb the fence, and I spoke to them. A little black girl said, "Is yo the manager of this here fence?" Of course, I was laughing so much within me that I couldn't answer her.

Let me describe the rest of my garden. In front, we had a white picket fence for division and beauty, and in front of that was a two foot strip of flowers with a row of brick for edging.

One day, I was lying on my back painting the bottom of the white fence. Soon I heard two boys talking behind the basket weave fence. They were unaware as I crawled over to the fence, stood up quickly, and said in a soft voice, "What are you boys doing here?" They were so surprised they about jumped out of their skins! They knew they were not supposed to climb the fence as I had told them many times. They said they were sorry and I replied, "I understand what it is like to be your age, and remember what I was like then. But one day, I asked Jesus to come into my life, and He changed me." Then Louie, the 14 year old, said he would like to talk to me about that. I told them I would love to, but they would have to come around by way of the street. To my surprise they came.

Louie began the conversation by saying a classmate of his had just died, and he had heard of the death of one of our neighbors recently, and for that reason was very much concerned about death. I explained that they could have Jesus in their hearts, have eternal life, and go to be with Him in heaven when they died. They both accepted the Lord. The next day their mother who, unbeknown to me, was a Child Evangelism worker, called and said how happy she was that I had led Louie to the Lord, and that he had really changed. What joy this brought to my heart.

A few weeks later, we thought there was a mouse in our basement window well. When Bernie went outside to investigate, he saw Louie looking around as though he had lost something. So he asked him what he was doing. He said he had lost his gerbil, and was looking for him. Bernie told him there was something in our window well and he was welcome to come and see if that's what he was looking for. It was his gerbil, and Louie said, "I was praying I would find him!"

Ministry in the U.S.

I was a good farmer that year with my garden in the backyard. I had also painted the white trim on the windows of our house, and it was done by the time Bernie returned from Seattle. Then he put up the outside frames. I got the worst end of that deal!

Paul felt the Lord was leading him into the field of Christian school administration. During the summer, he did some practice teaching at a nearby high school. It was a special joy to have him home. In the fall, he matriculated in Tennessee Temple University for a master's degree in school administration.

Paul motored up from Tennessee for Christmas of 1975 in his little Toyota, but had to leave before New Year.. Karen and Dave had just come home on furlough. A good imagination would be sufficient to picture a happy family reunion. We had hoped to have a photo of the four of us, but a robber had other designs! Not that he was interested in the Holritz great picture taking, but our cameras were worth quite a bit. After a five hour absence from our home on December 23, we returned to find our house had been thoroughly burglarized. Even PBA's safe had been broken, but not opened. What shocked us was our robber "friends" took our phone number, and were "kind enough" to call us later pretending to be the police saying they had caught the robbers, and gave us a number to call. To our dismay, it was the Sears building in Chicago! When we told the police what had happened, they said it was the robbers trying to heckle us. The experience with the robbers made us a bit uneasy because we were leaving for a month of meetings. Once again we were reminded that all we have belongs to Him, and we were confident God had some purpose for our good and His glory. When Morning Glory Church in Japan heard what had happened to us, they took up a special offering. It was just enough to cover the cost of replacing our camera equipment!

Chapter 4

Karen - Rhodesia

Karen's deputation trip was greatly blessed. However, the experience of having her suitcases stolen with all the clothes she had

made to be used in Rhodesia was most unpleasant! They were never recovered. The last weeks were filled with activities: shopping and packing Karen's outfit, commissioning service, visa and passport, compiling lists, farewells, etc. January 30, 1973, arrived and we were busy right up to the last minute so that we scarcely had time to think about Karen's departure. As the inspector went through her hand baggage, We couldn't help but laugh when he exclaimed, "The Lord never taught a woman, there is a limit to what a handbag can carry!" We walked the long isle to the plane with tears in our eyes. At the same time, there was a tremendous sense of joy. This was the hour we had prayed about even before she was born. There would be many adjustments as Karen began language study, and later her service in a rather lonely and primitive area of Africa. "We've a cablegram for you from Rhodesia," came a voice over the phone. Then a reassuring message, "Arrived safely in Rhodesia. Love, Karen."

Conditions in Rhodesia were ominous. An MK (missionary kid) brought us this firsthand report: A couple of months ago, terrorist activities were stepped up, and the attacks became more brutal, killing not only whites, but also blacks, including women and children. In the still of the night, rifle shots could be heard, and some nights there was no sleep for staff at TEAM's hospital as they were busy treating the wounded. Missionaries were no longer able to travel at night, and were advised to use an MAF (Missionary Aviation Fellowship) plane during the day. Three hundred school children and a priest were captured by the terrorists. Shortly after that, the government warned TEAM that the same thing was about to take place at their high school. The station was evacuated, but later they were able to return. Karen wrote that she went to the clinic to be of help.

The black people were terrified, and the Christians begged the missionaries to stay, as their presence was such a comfort to them. Karen wrote that the Lord had given her peace of heart in staying, and that she believed this was where the Lord wanted her. She advised in her letter sent with the MK that this information not be mentioned publicly or in letters to the field lest their position be jeopardized. So far, they have not tried to bother the missionaries as they are not politically involved. The government imprisoned the black cook from TEAM's language school (where Karen was) as he was found to be heavily involved in terrorist activities. The government was surprised that the missionaries had not been poisoned! The whole thing is communistically inspired, and all the weapons they had found were from Russia and China.

We had to learn patience – mail wasn't as fast from Rhodesia as it was from Japan. In early 1974, when we heard that Karen was ill, we felt so helpless, but realized that since she had been committed to the Lord, she was His responsibility. Karen had several attacks of fever which were finally diagnosed as toxoplasmosis – a big name for a small parasite that gets into the blood stream, and raises havoc with the whole system. She responded well to treatment, and was working again. The situation in Rhodesia continued to deteriorate! Several Christian nationals had been threatened or murdered! The terrorists had promised an increase in their activities.

Although Karen's schedule was very busy in 1975, but she enjoyed her ministry and started a Bible study among the women nursing students. The situation in Rhodesia was hard to understand and no one seemed to know just what the political changes meant. We heard that TEAM's hospital had been attacked by 20 armed terrorists. Praise God no one was injured.

We had some very exciting news from Karen. She announced her engagement to Dr. David Drake, the surgeon at the mission hospital. Karen and Dave wanted to marry soon, but this would not be possible because he was the only doctor at the hospital and there was no one to give him relief for a few days. Earlier, the terrorists had held Dave at bayonet point for forty-five minutes demanding money, but he refused – and lived to tell about it!

Karen and Dave's Wedding

We were not able to go to Rhodesia when Karen and Dave were married, but Dorothy Strom, wife of the field chairman, Wilfred Strom, was most gracious and wrote us a description of the activities of that day.

We want to share the letter which she wrote.

October 24, 1975
Dear Mr. & Mrs. Holritz and Paul:

Just a few hours ago, my husband had the privilege of escorting your precious Karen down the aisle of the church, on your behalf, and to give her in marriage to Dave. While the excitement lingers and the memories are fresh I want to share my view of the day with you and I know Karen will be sharing hers just a little later.

There were the usual hair appointments, etc. in the morning and then the excitement came upon us as we enjoyed a cold lunch together and started dressing. We began early enough to be able to enjoy it and to have ample time for pictures ---all went according to schedule and there were volumes of photos taken preparing and leaving for the church in the decorated car and arrival at the church. As we worked it out, Judy Everswick drove

Chapter 4

the bridal car, and to several pedestrians, Judy would blow the horn and Karen would wave. The African pedestrians were especially pleased by such attention from the bride. I followed two cars behind with Ann Britt, and we got the benefit of the excited reactions.

Right on the dot of 2:30 p.m., I felt very honored to be escorted down the aisle, acting as the bride's mother, to begin the celebration of "love and joy." When I was seated, Myrl Driedger gathered our thoughts together in worship to the Lord in her solo, "O Lord Most Holy." It was just like Karen and Dave wanted – the Lord received our thoughts and attention first.

With this spirit prevailing, the groom and his groomsmen entered from the left front of the church. Each of the girls looked charming in their matching dresses and the little girls with their baskets of flowers were very sweet without distracting our thoughts of receiving the bride. Karen's dress and veil (which she made) could not have been prettier, and the polyester crepe was such ideal material for not wrinkling on the drive to the church on the warm, sunny clear day that the Lord gave us. She looked so fresh, unaffected, and beautiful. Wilfred brought her to the front and Dave had walked over and Wilfred then said, "Dave, on behalf of her parents, who would love to be with us today but who are with us in thought and prayer, it is my privilege to give you Karen's hand in marriage."

The whole ceremony was simple enough to be sincere, but expressive enough to be dignified and meaningful. In all that was done, it came through loud and clear that it was Karen's and Dave's earnest desire that the Lord be glorified through their united lives.

Don Hoyt did a good job of getting many shots at the church, so I feel confident you will have quite a complete picture. There were also formal poses after the ceremony. This gave the TEAM ladies opportunity to get the details arranged for the reception on the hostel lawn...

Two nursing school students sang a duet, two of Mr. Holritz's numbers were played, telegrams were read—several from Japan—and this constituted the program... When you hear the tape of the reception you will hear the African students singing and that is when your call came through. Such a lovely conclusion to the reception...

Dave did quite well although he was limping some by the end of the day. (Dave seriously injured his back lifting a dying patient out of the mission plane a few weeks before the wedding.)

I should say what a joy it was to have Karen in our home for the few days prior to the wedding. We had great fun planning and joy in fellowship. Many times I asked the Lord to give you special grace as you accepted the Lord's plan for the wedding to be out here.

Sincerely in Him,
Dorothy Strom

In 1976, nine of Karen's nursing students were spared from death as the bus they had been riding was blown up five minutes from the hospital! Guerilla warfare was on the increase, and the hospital came under mortar fire. We were thankful that their marksmanship was poor and no one was hurt - another miracle of God's protection! The arrival of a doctor on the field made it

Chapter 4

possible for Dave and Karen to come on furlough. They arrived shortly before Christmas, well and happy, though a bit tense having lived in constant danger to their lives. They were overwhelmed by the abundance and all we had to enjoy as Americans. They were not certain of their plans, but would be working in a hospital during their furlough in order to gain further knowledge in their field of medicine.

Dave and Karen asked us to be their guests for Christmas in 1977. Paul invited a certain "friend" to our house for part of the Christmas holidays. One evening, Paul and his "friend" came to us with stars in their eyes saying they had a special announcement to make. That's right, Paul's "friend" was of the lovelier gender, and they showed us the diamond Paul had just put on the hand of Kathy DeBell! Paul had met Kathy at Tennessee Temple the previous year and they had been dating ever since. A summer wedding was planned. They were both teaching school in Chattanooga, looking forward to service for the Lord on some mission field.

PBA Japan's US Ministry Continued 1978 ~ 1981

Radio- Bernie

PBA faced a crisis. Dr. Akira Hatori had recovered from his heart attack in January, 1978, but later was hospitalized with internal bleeding! Junji, who was planning to come back to assist his brother, was not able to find a replacement for his pastorate in Nagoya, nor could we find housing for him in Tokyo, making it impossible for him to come.

In answer to prayers, the Lord raised up many new PBA friends and supporters during 1978, as well as one more person for the office and two new members for our Board of Directors. We thanked the Lord for a little respite before my '79 meetings which took me to Washington, DC, Texas, Michigan, and Ohio. Jeanette went with me to Alberta and Manitoba, Canada in June.

Another highlight was the production of a new stereo record in 1979. Several years ago a dear pastor friend, Bro. Joe West, said, "I wish someone would make a record of just songs about missions." Then another friend further challenged us by composing a mission song about Japan, and *"Tell Them of One"* became the

title song of the record. We prayed that God would use it to speak to people about the need of doing that which is near to the .heart of God – winning lost men, women, boys, and girls around the world for Christ. The record was made at Grace Bible Church along with their choir, instruments and ensemble.

Not until we prepared the fiscal year report did we realize that the Lord had enabled us to send 43% more to Japan last year than the year before. A few highlights from 1979 in PBA Japan: 21,500 letters and cards received; about 700 per month came from junior and senior high school students who listened to our youth program by shortwave from Guam; 15 people were saved through summer camp and 68 through the Christmas rallies. Several of Dr. Hatori's messages were printed in tract form and 377,000 were sold in Christian book stores; research and preparation for the new 13 week TV series was completed, the pilot program was done by June 1, and the rest of the series by January 1980.

On the home front, a little over a year ago, we had began a three minute daily program to be aired here in the States for the purpose of generating prayer for the total mission scene in Japan. It was on thirteen stations as sustained (free) time. The Lord gave us more opportunities to represent PBA than we ever had before. Our schedule for the next four months of 1980 was very heavy. We were encouraged by a large grant from a Christian foundation which enabled us to expand the TV outreach. It was a costly venture, but we believed it would be productive as well.

If I were Abraham Lincoln, I would say, "Three decades, one year and nine months ago, our family steamed into Yokohama harbor." One year later, we took part in founding Pacific Broadcasting Association. In October, 1981 we celebrated PBA's 30th anniversary with meetings in Los Angeles, Seattle, and Chicago. Dr. Hatori, our radio pastor, and his wife along with Steve Tygert, our Japan director, took part in all of the meetings. Jeanette

Ministry in the U.S.

and I were challenged again as we were privileged to have the Hatoris in our home for ten days. We talked Japanese, ate Japanese food -- it was almost like being back in Japan.

What a surprise it was, when at the Chicago banquet, Dr. Hatori presented us with a silver tray with the inscription, "Commemorating 30 years of service with PBA," and also a leather brief case. We will long remember that occasion.

Family

Bernie seemed to enjoy visiting hospitals! On July 20, 1978, he had surgery to remove cartilage from under the kneecap. He made remarkable recovery.

Our Chicago winter set a record snow fall and sub zero temperatures. We literally had to dig ourselves out! It made us wish we had planned a series of meetings in Florida, Arizona, or California—or better still the Bahamas!

Chapter 4

Christmas was quiet and pleasant at the Holritz household, though we missed Dave and Karen, as they visited Dave's relatives in Minnesota. Paul and Kathy arrived from Kokomo, IN, and were with us until the 28th. The activities of the week included ice skating, (for all but Jeanette who is still too much Texan) time around the piano with Kathy, who is an excellent pianist, some work projects, and eating (of course.)

In June, 1980, the children planned a belated get together for our 35th wedding anniversary. It was the first time Bradley and Nathan could play together.

Each spring we rototilled our garden in preparation for planting, but this year the "tilling" went a little deeper! The city replaced the flood and sanitary sewer main which meant digging a trench 10 feet wide and 19 feet deep right through the middle of our garden! They had been at it two months and weren't finished yet. So Jeanette said, "That's the end of my gardening for this year."

Jeanette's Brother

One of my brothers in Texas was killed in a single car accident in June because he was drunk; I went down to attend the funeral.

It was a sad occasion, and after the funeral, my family was sitting in a circle in the living room. Here is what happened. My father started bragging that he didn't drink (although he did on occasion) and therefore he was not responsible for Donnie's death. At that point I could stand it no longer and got down on my knees in front of him and said, "And what have you taught your boys, Daddy? You have taught them to curse continually, and other ungodly actions." I think my daddy would have struck me if the others hadn't been there. The next morning at breakfast I apologized to my father and said, "Although what I said was the truth, I should have talked to you privately."

An Update - Bernie

Forty years ago this month, (January, 1981) I walked down the aisle of a rescue mission in Fargo, ND, to accept Jesus as my Savior. These have been great years. He gave me a wonderful wife, led us into His service, gave us faithful prayer warriors, and in addition, God has blessed us with two children who have Christian mates and have been called into the Lord's service as well.

Karen & Dave

On Jan. 2, 1978, the Drakes boarded the plane for Rhodesia to relieve the doctor out there so that he could have a rest. As planned, the Drakes came back to the States in March, leaving a very precarious situation. The massacre of eight missionaries and four children took place just one hour from where TEAM's hospital is located.

It was great having Dave and Karen home on furlough. Though they didn't live in Wheaton, we talked to them by phone occasionally, and when they had meetings in our direction, they stopped to see us. (A lot different from when they lived in Rhodesia.) Dave studied at a medical school in Michigan, and then took some very difficult examinations. They had a rough furlough with everything so unstable: a few weeks in our area, three weeks in Michigan, two months of travel in deputation, and the last two months in Pontiac, Mich.

The Drakes also thrilled us with the news that come December, 1979, they too would be presenting us with a grandchild. (A few months earlier Paul and Kathy had told us of their expected arrival.) Imagine becoming grandparents twice in one year! In 1980, the situation in Rhodesia (now called Zimbabwe) was still precarious. So the mission advised Dave and Karen not to return to the field just yet. The elections would be held in a month so they were waiting to see what effect that would have on the situation. In the meantime, Dave was asked to go to Thailand to work with a medical mission team. Karen stayed in Ann Arbor, MI, to take care of Bradley, who had been diagnosed as having diabetes, and continue work on her master's degree at the University of Michigan. Jeanette spent a couple of weeks with Karen to help while Dave was away.

Dave no sooner returned from Thailand, than a call came from Zimbabwe asking him "to come as soon as possible" to survey the mission's medical outreach, and determine what was needed to resume that ministry. It appeared the medical work would be re-opened. Dave came back from Zimbabwe to coordinate with the mission, and was home for Christmas, but left for Zimbabwe a few days later. Karen remained to finish her last quarter of her master's degree in nursing which would be of great help in Zimbabwe. It also seemed wise that Bradley have a longer adjustment to his diabetic condition before returning to the field.

Paul & Kathy

Paul finished the academics for his master's degree and all that remained was his thesis. But in the meantime, he ran out of finances and took a temporary construction job in Ohio before re-

Ministry in the U.S.

turning to Chattanooga to finish his writing. He too had some major decisions to make. As parents, we would like to figure out all the answers for our children, but we realized how inadequate we were. God, their Heavenly Father, was the One Who could help them, and we committed them to His perfect direction.

Paul and Kathy had a beautiful wedding on June 3^{rd,} in Kirkland, WA. All but Dave was there. The whole service was a testimony to the Lord, and we received a wonderful daughter. Paul and Kathy returned to Chattanooga in order for Paul to complete his master's degree while Kathy continued teaching. In August, they moved to Kokomo, IN, where they both taught in a Christian school. They wanted a couple years of practical work before going to the field.

How do you adequately describe what it is like to be a grandparent? It's utterly impossible – unless you are one! As Jeanette and I looked at Nathan Andrew, we asked ourselves, "Is he really that beautiful? (He'll forgive us for using that term for a boy.) Or was it because he was our grandson?" At any rate, we were

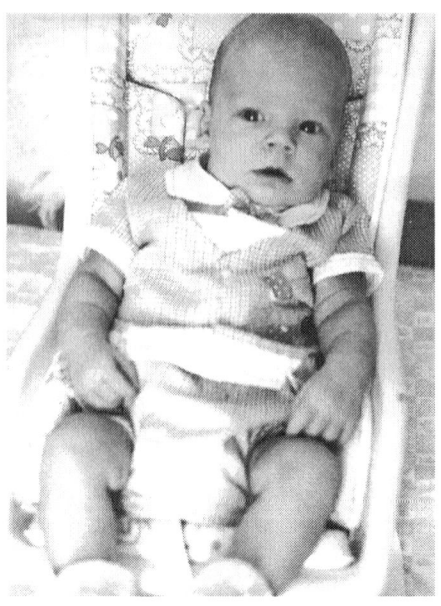

Chapter 4

thankful to our Heavenly Father for the gift of a healthy boy that the Lord gave us on August 23, 1979, and we prayed that God would make him like the Nathan and Andrew of the Scriptures. Paul and Kathy not only had a new responsibility of being parents, but Paul was made principal of Temple Baptist Christian School, in Kokomo, IN.

Responsibility in the Christian school as well as in their home church kept Paul and Kathy well occupied along with Nathan, who was six months old. Their burden for the mission field was mounting, and they planned to attend the mission candidate school of ABWE (Association of Baptists for World Evangelism) in New Jersey. Their interest was Japan, but they wanted to be sure of God's will.

We had been jumping for the phone each time it rang anticipating news from Paul and Kathy in Kokomo, IN, ready to ask the question, "Is it a boy or girl?" At last, on Thursday evening, January

8, 1981 Paul called to tell us that Jason Marc had arrived, and weighed nine pounds five ounces! (That's practically full grown, isn't it?) So we have three grandsons. The Christian school where Paul and Kathy had been serving found a replacement for Paul so they began full-time deputation.

TEAM'S SOUTHEAST REPRESENTATIVE – 1981 ~ 1992

Accepting TEAM'S Invitation

After the celebration of PBA'S 30th anniversary in September, 1981, we were faced with a major decision. TEAM asked us if we would consider becoming their Southeast Representative. After much prayer, and reading of the Word, we were assured of the Lord's direction, and accepted the call from TEAM. We were excited about the opportunity of sharing the needs of a worldwide ministry.

Our move to Lilburn, Georgia

Our first task was to sell our house at a time houses were not selling! After that, we could move to Georgia which seemed to

be central for working in the states of Georgia, North and South Carolina, Tennessee, Florida, and Alabama. But between the time of giving our answer to TEAM, and our arrival in Lilburn, there were many battles to fight, lessons to learn, and bridges to cross. We sensed the under girding of prayer. As we look back, there was a verse that summarizes what took place. "The mind of man plans his way, but the Lord directs his steps." Prov. 16:9. From the beginning, we were sure the Lord wanted us in the Atlanta area, but we needed a place to stay while we looked for housing. We saw God's provision through a contact of Mrs. Lankford's daughter, Carol. A wonderful Christian lady, Mrs. Heralson, let us stay in her home, fix our own meals, and complete freedom to come and go as we needed. We made two survey trips, but the only area we had peace about was east of the city. Our son, Paul, had suggested that we find a house that would be near a good church which would become our church home. But how would we find that in a short time?

We also wanted a contractor to inspect the house we had found before we made the final decision. In March, on our second trip to Atlanta, we discovered that Mrs. Heralson's son-in-law was a contractor! He not only gave his approval, but said that the house was worth more than market price. Then he invited us to visit his church (Killian Hill Baptist) which he said, "is just a few miles from this house." The first Sunday we visited, and heard the preacher (Bro. Mike Riley), we were sure this was to be our church home – another assurance from the Lord.

We signed a contract to buy the house with a three months contingency clause, that we sell our house in Wheaton first. The problem was, it was a buyer's market! Everyone who was interested in our house said the same thing; they would have to sell their house first. It was like falling dominos, only we could not get the first domino to fall! These months became a time of searching our hearts and motives. The Bible became more meaningful and precious to our hearts. Questions came, not only from ourselves, but from dear ones who were concerned; however, God gave us courage to go on.

To add to our dilemma, suddenly Bernie had a back problem that sent him to the hospital for ten days. During this time, Jeanette was busy trying to sell our house which she felt was too much for her to handle. One night during Bernie's absence, Jeanette could not sleep, and poured out her heart to the Lord. In the hospital, although she didn't know it, Bernie was going through the same battle. The next day, a couple came to look at the house. They seemed pleased, but as they left, the dog across the street started barking, and they commented on it. Jeanette thought to herself, "Well, that's the end of that!" But the lady called back and said they were interested, "Put our name in the pot." Bernie was released from the hospital and early the next morning the husband came back, unannounced, saying, "The Lord told me to get over there and buy that house." He said he wanted to submit a bid. That was July 1, 1982. A week later, we signed the contract with the closing to be the 22nd. But then, we learned that the prospective buyer's money was tied up in an estate court! Being Christians, they asked us to pray with them, that their problems would be settled so they could meet the closing date. After much prayer, the buyers were able to get their funds for the transaction.

When we called Lilburn, we learned that the house was still available. We began packing.

Although the doctor had said Bernie was to do no lifting for six weeks, the Lord touched his back, and he was able to do all kinds of work. The movers had everything out of the house on the 28th. An added blessing was a dear Christian brother had his men from Service Master completely clean the house for us. We arrived in Lilburn, had the closing on August 4th; five days after our contingency had expired! From the time we arrived and started moving into our new house, our hearts were at rest knowing we were where God wanted us. Meetings had opened up from October through February. (We even had a date for February, 1984!) Bernie was anxious to get started working with the churches and pastors in the seven states, helping our TEAM missionaries and MKs, as well as start a missions program on radio stations in this area.

Other Happenings

Another milestone in our lives was to have both of our children on the mission field. Dave, Karen, and little Bradley returned to Zimbabwe in June. Paul, Kathy, Nathan, and little Jason arrived in Tokyo on December, 1982, for their first term of service. The miraculous supply of their needs brought back memories of His provision for our first departure to Japan.

We were greatly moved by the severe illness and death of Bob Root, the man who took Bernie's place in PBA, as well as the sudden death of Lester Roloff, a man who had encouraged us to go into the ministry and stood by us all these years.

On November 30, the doctor discovered a lump on Bernie's prostate gland which he was sure was cancerous, but said, "To prove myself wrong, I want to take a biopsy," and scheduled it for Dec. 9. This became a time of heart searching, and much prayer. As we waited to be taken to surgery, we saw a spectacular sunrise. Suddenly, its rays caught the five storied glass covered building on Stone Mountain making it appear as though the whole building were aflame and two or three times its actual size. The event lasted about 20 minutes. We thought nothing more of it until after we learned the results of the biopsy. When Bernie came out of the recovery room, Jeanette was waiting to tell him the doctor's preliminary report. "I found stones, but took specimens anyway." This meant another long twenty four hour wait before receiving the pathologist's report, "Biopsy benign!"

Then I remembered a verse that had blessed my heart before leaving Wheaton. "That our God may count you worthy of your calling, and fulfill every desire for goodness and the work of faith with power <u>in order that the name of our Lord Jesus may be glorified in you and you in Him</u> according to the grace of our God and the Lord Jesus Christ." II Thes. 1:11 & 12. I compared it to the blazing spectacle that we had seen before going to surgery. The response of my heart was, "God, in this life you have given back to me, glorify Thyself like that in me and I in You. May it not be a momentary flash, but a life long commitment!"

"It's a girl!" What a delightful bit of news that reached us by cablegram on the morning of December 6. It simply said:

"Rejoicing in the Lord. Heather Michelle arrived on Dec. 5 at 10:15 a.m., 8 and a half pounds. Dad delivered. Dave" So now we had one granddaughter and three grandsons. Needless to say, we'd like to have them all near us, but at the same time we were delighted that they were where God wanted them.

It was 1983, and we couldn't thank the Lord enough for the home we lived in, as well as our church. God had done something special for us in both of these. Already the new ministry had been very satisfying. Although we had several mission conferences in which to speak and sing, we had concentrated on visiting pastors in the area to get acquainted. We knew the Lord had gone before us as we had good reception. Bernie enjoyed lining up meetings for other TEAM missionaries and appointees in the southeast. How satisfying to hear that these churches had taken on the support of some of them.

Specific requests for personnel had come from the field. For example, our daughter and son-in-law in Zimbabwe were hurting for nurses. The Lord enabled us to find a lady to go out for six months, (We wish we could tell you how the Lord brought all this together.) Then a request came for some carpenters for Brazil. The Lord enabled us to find a family to go for a year to help build a Bible camp for the mission. We also tried to find a doctor for the hospital in United Arab Emirates, but never could. In the process, however, we gained a lot of good contacts for future needs. What a privilege to work with so many pastors, churches, missionaries, appointees, MKs, and missionary parents. We needed God's Spirit upon us so that we would minister effectively for Him.

This year, 1983, in a fresh way we have learned the importance of giving thanks. We were especially aware that the Lord had sustained our health. Bernie was on medication, but the doctor was pleased with his progress. (Our doctor was Jewish, and we had been witnessing to him.) Six weeks following surgery, with the doctor's consent, we flew to Texas, California, and Arizona for ten days of meetings. We were home two days, and then drove to Indiana for another mission conference. The whole month of November had been full.

Karen and Dave wrote that Heather, our only granddaughter, (one year old) was a source of joy and delight to them. Bradley's diabetes was under control, for which we were grateful, but his parents needed much discernment in caring for him. A report from our mission read, "The Karanda Hospital is experiencing unusual blessings from the Lord, but there are serious personnel shortages."

After finishing final language requirements, Paul and Kathy moved to the southernmost island of Kyushu near the city of Kagoshima. Their letters and pictures had helped us live this experience right with them. They were getting acquainted with neighbors. On October 9th, they started a church in their new home. In November, Nathan and Jason would have either a sister or brother to join them!

On occasion, our children had asked if there were any plans to visit them. The church we started in Japan, had requested a visit from us, and we also wanted to see the new PBA facilities. We asked the Lord for His direction in these matters.

We had a unique opportunity of teaching a series of messages on missions in a church. It was wonderful to see the response both in and out of the class. On Feb. 3, 1984, along with three other mission reps, Bernie had the privilege of taking part in a seminar on "Present Opportunities on the Mission Field," for one hundred fifteen college and career young people (never had literature been taken from our display table as they did.) Several asked for application forms for TEAM's summer missions program. Bernie also had the privilege of participating in the annual mission conference of the Southeastern Bible College in Birmingham, AL. (About 90% of the alumni are in full time Christian work!)

We received word from Japan that on February 19th Paul and Kathy's third son, Joshua Luke, was born. (That's quite a name to live up to!) All went well and we were very thankful.

We were very busy in conferences and meetings from March through most of May. In the midst of these meetings, we had a visit from Bro. and Mrs. Iide, pastor of Morning Glory Church.

Chapter 4

They were on their way to visit their missionaries in South America. We were thankful for the ministry the Lord had given us these last two years. The southeast had been a difficult area for faith missions such as TEAM, but the attitude was changing, and we were seeing doors and hearts opened. We were challenged to find personnel to fill slots on the mission field – some for just a few short weeks, others for longer periods.

We had also witnessed to five of our neighbors, trying to point them to the Savior. Jeanette had the joy of leading one of the ladies, Joyce Betz, to the Lord. Thus began a wonderful series of miracles that only God could have orchestrated. Eventually Bob, though adamantly opposed at first, became a godly husband and father, not only caring for his family, but reaching out to others through his home Bible class. Their son, Brent was also saved. They have become some of our dearest friends.

In October, TEAM called a special medical consultation conference for the administrative staff of all their hospitals. This meant that Dave and Karen had to be present. When they arrived in the states, they called and asked "Mom, can you come to Wisconsin to take care of Brad and Heather while we attend the sessions?" Guess what she answered? You're right, she went. Thus she saw our new granddaughter before I did, but we did have six packed full days with the Drakes here before they returned to Zimbabwe. Naturally our visit with the Drakes made us lonesome for Paul, Kathy, and the three boys, one which we had never seen. Jason had serious asthma problems and had to be rushed to the hospital on occasion.

We had been praying about the possibility of visiting the Drakes on their field when we received an invitation to be the speaker for the Zimbabwe field conference. One of our navy friends, not knowing of the invitation, made a sizable contribution toward such a project. So we stepped out in faith, believing God would supply the rest of the finances. Mission headquarters sanctioned the trip, and suggested we also visit some of TEAM's other fields as well. So the project grew to a seven week trip. We left on November 27. Our first stop was Spain where we stayed in the home of one our missionaries and enjoyed getting acquainted with their family. When the parents introduced us as "Uncle and Auntie" (which is usually what the children called the missionaries) their little boy looked at us for a moment and then said, "That's no uncle and auntie; that's a grandma and grandpa!" We also saw the work around Madrid, attended the dedication of a new church building, and talked with one of the outstanding evangelists of the country. With the change of government from a dictatorship to more of a democratic form, new liberties had come to Protestant missions. There had been an influx of missionaries and they were praying for seven new couples for church planting.

We left Spain, and thirteen hours later were in Zimbabwe – our first time in the Southern Hemisphere. Our winter clothes were far too heavy for midsummer! Daughter, Karen, and her husband, Dave, and their two children, Bradley and Heather, were at the airport to meet us. We left immediately for their hospital in Karanda. It would be difficult to describe our feelings after leaving the modern city of Harare, and driving, for what seemed endless miles, through its villages of grass huts, finally to round the curve, and catch a glimpse of the hospital and dwelling complex set against an indescribably blue sky with low mountains in the distance. Truly we felt overwhelmed and at a loss for words.

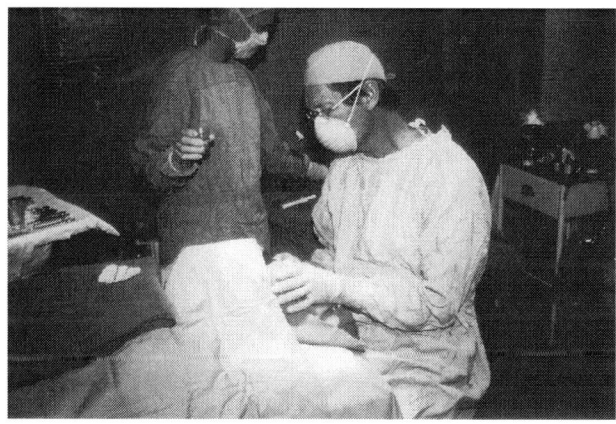

This, in fact, was what we had prayed for all these years. The next day, Bernie watched Dave and Karen perform a double cataract surgery!

Returning to Harare, we began a long journey by car to visit missionaries and pastors who were in the thick of the battle for souls. To us, Zimbabwe was a paradox; wonderful opportunities to preach, teach, and plant churches in a country whose government professes to be Communist. God was building His church there. Yes, there were dangers and opposition. Even so, new missionaries were arriving on the field.

Then came the time for the field conference. What an awesome responsibility to be the speaker! These were missionaries who had been in the thick of the battle, and they needed encouragement. Bernie spoke from the book of Philippians. We felt the Lord's enabling throughout the time.

While on our survey trip from Zimbabwe to South Africa, we noted the extreme difference between the two countries. South Africa was more highly developed. One could buy anything there. The effect of the apartheid government is seen everywhere. Yet there were changes taking place. We saw TEAM's ministry among the Africans (black), the Indians, and the colored (mixed race.) God was at work in all three of these groups as well as among the Europeans. Again, we saw the need of more missionaries to do church planting.

How blessed it was to return to Zimbabwe, and spend Christmas with the family. Grandchildren are a wonderful creation of God! Jeanette enjoyed playing with Bradley in the sandbox. He would make up stories and enact them. Heather enjoyed the baby buggy we brought for her, and was pushing it all over the house. One day her mother put her to bed a bit early and she stood in her bed crying out, "Yuki! Yuki! Yuki!" until she finally fell asleep. Bradley was so excited to tell us about the black mamba (snake) that got into their attic, and how his father, Dave, had shot it with a shotgun. We were much concerned about Bradley, and we've learned what it's like to care for a young boy with diabetes.

After leaving Zimbabwe, we traveled to Italy. We came from 95 degree to 15 degree weather! It was quite a shock. We were told this was the worst winter since 1962. We didn't get out much, but we did see TEAM's church in Forley. Our mission had only been in Italy for two years, so everyone was still struggling to learn the language and how to make contact with the people. We have some very capable missionaries, and they too are calling for more personnel.

Our arrival in France was two days late because of the heavy snow in Italy! But the missionaries had arranged a meaningful time for us. Churches were growing in size and number. We were particularly blessed to hear how God had undertaken in behalf of two churches to provide locations and buildings in one place in spite of the opposition of the Mayor.

1985

The survey trip we had envisioned had now become history. Jeanette and I traveled thousands of miles by plane and car. Although we had been in dangerous areas and had numerous changes in time, climate, and food, neither of us had any health problems during the seven weeks of our trip.

On arriving home, we found dear friends from our church in Atlanta to welcome us and a refrigerator full of food that they had brought. While we read the letters that had come during our absence, we learned that the brother who had paid the bulk of the funds needed for our trip had suddenly been called into the presence of our Lord. He had been a dear brother since navy days.

For ten days, we had the joy of housing David Chettiar, an Indian brother from South Africa. He made a statement that challenged our hearts, "Information provides fuel for intercessory prayer." We were privileged to introduce him to six churches in this area.

God used him to waken the hearts of many for missions, salvation, and dedication. Some of the churches had never had anyone from TEAM before, even so, one of the churches took on one third of his support.

Mendozas

A young Christian couple whom we've known since we've been in Liburn gave us their car. We thank the Lord for this Delta 88 which was just like new. This couple blessed us and our children in so many ways, even giving our son a car also. They became just like family and we dearly loved their children. We began to be referred to us as, "Aunt Jeanette and Uncle Bernie." We will never forget the night when we were with the Mendozas in the hospital at 3 a.m. and Greg came down the hall shouting, "It's a girl. It's a girl." Jeanette had special fun times with Audrey. One day Audrey asked Jeanette to tell her the story of *Little Red Riding Hood*, to which she replied, "I'm just too tired and can't remember it." Then Audrey said, "I'm going to tell you the story so that you can remember it and the next time I come you can tell the story to me!"

Earlier in the spring, we had a visit from one of the members of our church in Japan. This man had been led to the Lord by our son, Paul, when he was in Japan as a short term missionary. Mr. Isobe was a leader in the church and wanted to visit churches in America to see how they operated.

We were seeking to find at least one doctor and several nurses for the hospital in Zimbabwe. It was not only difficult to find personnel, but also to obtain entry permits. A nurse who had her support and entry permit, was suddenly struck with a serious illness which canceled her going! However, the Lord called an older couple to go to Trinidad to take the place of a TEAM missionary coming back for furlough. The Lord wonderfully supplied their support in a very short time. Sometime ago, we intro-

Chapter 4

duced one of our doctors working in United Arab Emirates to a church in Atlanta. We thought the contact was unfruitful, but they called saying they had voted to take on a sizable amount of Dr. Salem Barghout's support.

Family, Health, and Ministry

What a thrill it has been to pick up the phone and talk to Paul, Kathy, and the grandchildren here in the U.S. It had been four years since we last saw them. They planned to visit us between deputation meetings. They were scheduled to speak in 36 churches in the four months they were on furlough!

There were also health needs. Bernie was placed on one week of complete voice silence due to extreme hoarseness. With medication, the doctor hoped it would be corrected. If not, further tests on his vocal cords would be necessary. We were concerned as his voice is very crucial to his ministry. After several sessions with the doctor, it was decided to do surgery on October 25th to remove a benign growth on his vocal cords. He was on another ten days of total voice rest. (His new verse for the year was, "study to be quiet." I Thess. 4:11) He was scheduled to be the soloist and emcee at TEAM's anniversary banquet Nov 8th. The doctor could not give clearance until he saw him on Nov. 1st.

TEAM has been relatively unknown in this part of the country, and yet we were delighted to have over 400 in attendance at the anniversary banquet in Atlanta. (The doctor finally gave permission for Bernie to emcee though he was somewhat hoarse.) This goodly number was due in part to the excellent banquet committee who, likewise burdened for missions, worked very hard to make this meeting a success. We thank God for each one who came, especially a number of busy pastors as well as potential mission candidates. One member of the banquet committee continued on as producer of a radio program called, *Radio Mission Prayer Band*, for which Bernie was the speaker. It was a weekly

Ministry in the U.S.

15 minute program, aired locally at present. If it goes well, Bible Broadcasting Network wants it on all their stations.

However, the succeeding weeks indicated that Bernie's voice was not improved by the surgery! An examination by another ENT revealed a small polyp on the right vocal cord, but did not advise surgery again. However, allergy tests were advised because his throat was aggravated by a constant postnasal drip. The second specialist wanted to try Bernie on further voice rest to see whether he would improve. Bernie's voice problem had been present almost nine months. We had wondered what lessons the Lord wanted us to learn from this, and were much concerned, as our future ministry was dependent upon the use of his voice for speaking and singing. Meetings planned for the Midwest in February had to be canceled.

Christmas was especially meaningful, as Paul, Kathy, and boys were with us. Bernie's fondest memories were of reading bed

time stories to our three grandsons, while Jeanette's was the cuddling of little Joshua – a stage in the lives of our other grandchildren we missed. After they were gone, we missed the patter of little feet, the rollicking with three lively boys, the hugs and kisses, and even the little finger marks on the coffee table! We were so glad Bernie's sister from Arizona, who was also visiting us for Christmas, could stay a few more days after Paul and family left for Japan via Seattle. The previous Christmas we were privileged to be in Africa with Dave, Karen, and the children; so God had been good to us.

Continuing Health Problems - Bernie

I had vocal surgery last October. Then on June 25, 1986, I had surgery again to correct a deviated septum (a crooked nose bone) and strip the vocal cords. Five days later, when the doctor pulled the rather leaf shaped tubes and packing from each nostril, Jeanette about flipped and I almost passed out. I could breathe like never before, and we hoped the cause of the postnasal drip, which constantly irritated the vocal cords, would be cleared up. Again there would be one month of total voice silence. The doctor told me not to expect too much when I first start to use my voice. It would take a couple of months before we would know the total results of the surgery. We believed we had done what the Lord wanted us to do. Whether I sang again or how well I would be able to speak was all in God's hands.

The time of total silence was hard for both of us. To others, living with a husband who cannot talk might be a relief. Jeanette found it frustrating trying to keep Bernie quiet! However, when she used his notes and put them into action, in addition to making telephone calls, she felt fulfilled.

With Jeanette's help, as well as others, we would have our hands full continuing to prepare for two all day seminars for pastors and mission committees, one in Atlanta, October 10, and the other in Birmingham, October 11. There were delegates from four states. This was a very large undertaking with three of our top men coming from TEAM Headquarters. A continuing project was the weekly missionary radio program. Bernie had recorded all the programs through the end of July, but would have

Ministry in the U.S.

to write the script for the month of August so that another missionary could do the speaking.

In the midst of this physical problem, we had the opportunity of calling a group of 24 doctors and nurses together to hear a challenge from one of TEAM's doctors from Nepal. We prayed the Lord would lead many of them to the mission field, either for a short term or as a career.

The months following the second vocal surgery were some of the most traumatic and yet some of our richest times spiritually. Two months after the surgery, the vocal therapist classified my condition as "voiceless," as I only had about 60% of my voice. For awhile it seemed like progress was one step forward and two backward!

Town East Baptist Church in San Antonio, Texas, asked us to participate in their first missionary conference, and we became their first missionaries. Then, twenty-five years later, they asked us to return for the anniversary of this occasion. At the same time, we visited three other supporting churches as well as Jeanette's folks.

Family

There had been much progress in Paul's ministry in Japan, but not without opposition from Satan. Their main request was for Japanese <u>men</u> to be saved. Letters from Dave and Karen in Zimbabwe have been encouraging as well. At last, they were able to obtain entry permits for some doctors and nurses, which enabled them to make plans for a much needed furlough.

On the 25th of October, I reached another milestone. I turned 65! No, we'weren't retiring. In spite of the number of health problems, we felt "there was still a lot of tread on the tires," and we wanted to work a few more years. As far as the mission's policy, we could stay until 70.

This Christmas was different. It could have been lonely, but we talked to Paul, Kathy, and boys in Japan, and received a telegram from Dave, Karen, and children in Zimbabwe. The Lord also gave us the opportunity to encourage a very dear family that was going through a time of sorrow.

My vocal condition had made progress, howbeit slow. (At least we thought so.) I had been preaching, but I could not sing solos. Perhaps that would be possible someday. I was still fighting an allergy that caused a sinus drain irritating my vocal cords.

1987

As a result of the Atlanta and Birmingham seminars the previous October, we were invited to do one in Florida, February 2. TEAM was also asked to participate in the Atlanta based Medical Missionary Fellowship.

I got a computer through TEAM for my office – a double disc 640k RAM with a letter style printer. How did Jeanette feel about this?

> "I must admit that I am amazed that 'an inanimate object' – though I question the use of those words in this case – could so completely invade our premises. It is almost like having another member of the family, only a rather cantankerous one with none of the Christian graces – somewhat touchy, oversensitive, and a perfectionist, that demands the same from anyone who dares to cross its path!
>
> "Once this temperamental intruder went on a pouting spell and hid an important piece of information

within its body works. After hours of searching, yea even days, Bernie inadvertently touched a rather sensitive nerve and in a moment of frenzied activity, it yielded forth the prized possession.

"Through all these testings, Bernie bravely stood his ground, refusing to be conquered. At the same time, desiring to 'live peaceably with all men,' (and creatures alike.) Bernie, with much patience, finally quieted 'The Thing' and perhaps even humbled it to the point of becoming a useful servant in the Holritz household."

Jeanette had surgery Feb. 5 to lift her brow and lids which had dropped so much that her vision was impaired. It was a three hour ordeal!

A tape from the Holritzes in Japan was encouraging. It amazed us the number of contacts they had as well as places to minister, but of the fourteen Christians in the church, all were women but one. They have asked the Lord to increase their number to 30 including at least five men.

The Drake's furlough began May 15. They needed adequate means of transportation, preferably a van.

TEAM's annual conference was the best ever. We were challenged to see the progress that had been made in places where the opposition had been strong. We also learned of visa problems such as in Irian Jaya where 60% of the missionaries were affected by new restrictions. TEAM announced the adding of three new fields: Mexico, Mozambique, and the Philippines. We had one of the largest enrollments for candidate school, but we needed to pray them out to the field.

Chapter 4

Family

Dave, Karen, Bradley, and Heather, back from Zimbabwe, spent a month with us before leaving for deputation. The Lord provided a large van for their travels. They were on the road continuously for the next few months.

Paul, Kathy, Nathan, Jason, and Joshua were doing well in Japan. Their co-workers were all on furlough. Paul was field chairman, as well as the added responsibility of camp director.

We had several projects going: establishing a medical mission fellowship in Atlanta, a children's missions VBS program which could also be used for church mission conferences, getting contacts for new and furloughed missionaries, and seeking missionary recruits.

Jeanette had had arthritic knee pains for about two years. Finally her right knee completely gave way. Three orthopedic doctors later, the diagnosis was the cartilage on one side of the knee was gone and it was bone on bone. Jeanette was unable to walk without a brace, and an electronic device to block the pain. She had quite a daily regimen – five or six leg strengthening exercises, ice packs, hot soak, etc. If that program was not successful, we were advised that she would have to have a very involved surgery that might not be successful.

Dave and Karen were with us before they returned to the field in October; thus they were with us the first and last months of their furlough. In between, they traveled over 20,000 miles! Bradley and Heather attended our church's school the last weeks they were here. One day, when Jeanette was doing her knee exercises, Heather came into the room and saw her. Jeanette would say, "Come on Grandma, get that knee up there; get that knee up there!" Heather began laughing and started doing the exercises with her.

One day when Jeanette was looking out the kitchen window watching Brad and Heather riding their bikes on our cement driveway. Shortly after they started, Heather stopped because her locket fell from her neck. Instantly, Brad dismounted his bike, picked up the locket, and gently put it back around her neck. We were not too surprised as Karen had written that Bradley not only watched over Heather, but also the Zimbabwean children.

Before they returned, Jeanette said to Heather, "Grandma is going to miss you so much when you go back to Zimbabwe." She responded, "Oh, don't worry, Grandma, I'll pray for you!"

Though we missed Paul, Kathy, and boys a great deal, their letters and tapes gave us much fuel for prayer. They, as well as our Japanese church, had been urging us to make a trip to Japan, but we had delayed due to our health and other factors. We prayed about a September date to coincide with the anniversary meetings of Paul and Kathy's church.

Chapter 4

Ministry

We participated in some very fruitful mission conferences in the area. Also, a special joy was to see a doctor and his wife, whom we had counseled, enter Bible school, make formal application to TEAM, and attended candidate school in June. They were seeking the mind of the Lord as to which of TEAM's hospitals they should apply. For a long time, Bernie had hoped to put on a banquet in Birmingham, but had never been successful. Now, however, we found a working committee and engaged Dr. Warren Wiersbe as speaker. We felt he would be a great blessing, not just for the banquet, but for the cause of missions in the Birmingham area. Our plan was for the spring of 1988.

The use of the computer (in spite of its obstinacy!) had helped Bernie to keep constant contact with the pastors and churches in this area enabling him to arrange meetings for missionaries on furlough, appointees, and visiting office staff. The response to his correspondence was encouraging. Although we had been frustrated by our physical afflictions, God had given us a ministry we might have missed, had we been well. Gen. 41:52b has taken on fresh meaning. We had answers to prayers for which we had waited many years.

Ministry in the U.S.

On April 22, 1988, Paul called from Japan that Jeremy Matthew had made his appearance. Now the Holritzes had a male quartet! Poor Kathy was alone among five boys!

Jeanette's Lung Surgery, Iwasaki and Winchell Visit

Jeanette was to have knee surgery, but before that, she had to have a pre-op examination. The doctor saw a golf ball size shadow on the left lung and said there would be no surgery done until we find out what that shadow was! She was put on some very strong medication to see if the growth would respond. When it didn't, the doctor said, "The growth must be removed immediately!" Surgery was on May 12th. After an eighteen inch incision, a part of the lung was removed. Before surgery, the doctor was sure it was cancer, but after the biopsy was completed, it proved to be an encapsulated TB growth that had been dormant for 30 years, probably contracted while we were missionaries in Japan. We were thankful that Jeanette's lungs had no signs of congestion, and were in excellent shape. After ten days in the hospital, three in ICU, she was entirely free of TB, but would have to remain on medication and have monthly examinations for the next nine months.

In July, we had a wonderful visit from our friends, Kitao and Fumiko Iwasaki. This visit seemed like a dream come true. We had eleven wonderful days to laugh, play, and pray together. Jeanette was still recovering from her lung surgery and, though her knee bothered her, she was able to get around. Four days after the Iwasakis left, Jeanette had arthroscopic surgery on her knee!

Chapter 4

Meetings were scheduled for Dr. Dick Winchell, our mission's General Director, Oct. 22nd through 26. He spoke in three churches, and two Bible colleges in the Atlanta area and also at a pastors' luncheon. From November 9-13, Bernie was to be the speaker for a mission conference in Jacksonville, FL.

Japan Visit Canceled

We looked forward to Nov. 18, with a great deal of anticipation. Our visas for Japan and Taiwan, as well as the "omiage" (gifts) we were taking to our friends and family, were in hand. We had found a travel agent that gave us the best schedule and price. All the arrangements were made with the folks in Japan and Taiwan. Jeanette had wrapped all the packages, and I had packed them in boxes ready for the plane. Ladies from our church in Lilburn had made some gifts we were to take to the ladies of Morning Glory Church for their annual Christmas gathering. Everything had to be ready before I was to go to Florida for a mission's conference, because we would only have three days after I returned. We were ready, BUT --- all the while we were making these preparations, Jeanette's knee worsened and mobility became more and more restricted.

Ministry in the U.S.

We had until October 31 to decide whether we would be able to make the trip. Because of the type of tickets we bought, we could not change the route or cancel without losing about 50% of what we had paid! We called Paul and found a problem had developed in their schedule which would limit the time they could spend with us. That, plus health factors, tipped the scales. We canceled our trip!

Florida Trip - Bernie

We felt badly for everyone involved, but most of all for our poor grandchildren! It was hard for them to understand why grandma and grandpa couldn't come. Having to repack all the boxes and mail them had not been in our plans. It took longer than we thought. As a result, it was "nip and tuck" getting ready to go to Jacksonville, Florida. Jeanette was unable to get around the house by herself, so we went together. The folks there had wanted her to come in the first place, so it worked out well.

This was the first conference in several years where I was to be the principal speaker. I spoke five times with no difficulties. In fact, my voice seemed to get stronger as the conference proceeded. It appeared that the Lord used the messages in the lives of several people as well. I felt like I was getting reactivated. My hopes were to be more involved in meetings in the future. The Lord used us in helping others to get into churches, and we did not want to neglect that either.

Early in April, 1989, Jeanette had bi-lateral knee replacements. Less than six weeks later, we were able to make the trip to Seattle for the Rep. Retreat, & TEAM's Annual Conference. There we met Paul, Kathy, and the four boys just home from Japan. Jeanette wasn't without pain, but she was able to move about quite freely with the use of a cane. Seven months later, Jeanette's left knee was better than the right. The problem was

Chapter 4

the doctor who performed the first knee surgeries should have done a total rather than a partial knee replacement. Recovery was much slower than had been anticipated. In some ways, there is more pain than before surgery, but the difference was she could walk whereas she couldn't before. Jeanette was thankful to be able to drive and shop once again.

After three and a half years, I was once again able to sing solos! The first time was at our mission's rep retreat. It was a moving experience for us as Kathy accompanied me and our TEAM-mates prayed. It was just as moving as when I sang at our home church when we returned from conference. Our pastor and his wife presented me with a beautiful plaque with the words paraphrased from Song of Solomon,

> "For lo the winter is past,
> The rain is over and gone,
> The flowers appear on the earth,
> And the time of singing has come."

The new people in church were surprised to hear my strong singing voice. What a miracle of God! I have had several more opportunities to sing and speak, though we have learned my speaking voice is much weaker than my singing voice. However, with a PA system, he is able to be understood.

Family News

We received some shocking news when we learned that Jason, Paul and Kathy's son, was in the hospital with a severe asthma attack; his lung capacity was so low the doctor was amazed that he even survived! Paul and family were planning to move to the southeast after Christmas to be near us, but the doctor was very adamant that to move him to another environment at this time would endanger his life. Of course, we were disappointed, as we had only seen them a few days since their furlough, and after an absence of four years we longed to have more time with them. Travel was expensive and time consuming, but it seemed our only hope of being together was to go to Seattle. Dave, Karen, and children plan to return to the States by summer, and we were hoping for a reunion. It had been eight years since we had been together as a family. We knew if God was in it, He'd make it possible.

Paul, Kathy, and boys moved to Denver, CO, to put Jason in a special hospital for asthmatics on July 9, 1990. The depth of the

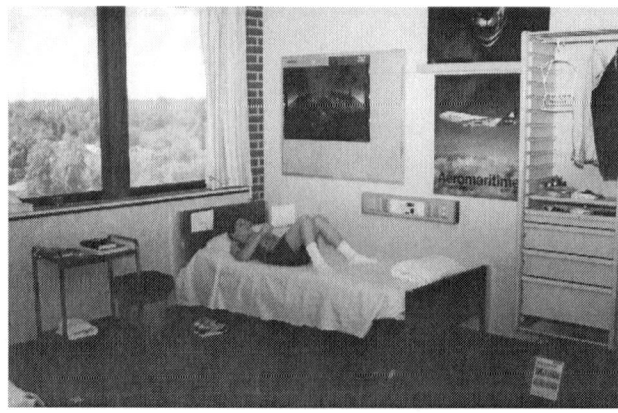

diagnosis as well as treatment were not available in Seattle. They were detained a year to give Jason time to stabilize. At that time, they would determine the next step. Meanwhile, they were considering deputation with an occasional trip to Japan. Dave, Karen, Bradley, and Heather arrived in Atlanta on July 13. They were in need of transportation; so lots of time was spent looking for a van. Seven days went quickly, but what a joy it was to read and play with Bradley and Heather. My, how they had grown! The Drakes were asked to consider a change in assignment which would be quite drastic on the whole family.

Anniversaries

1990 was TEAM's 100th anniversary. To celebrate the occasion, they were sponsoring banquets around the country. We had planned banquets in Atlanta and Macon, GA. Frank Boggs was

the soloist for the evening in Atlanta. Dick and Marg Winchell were with us and Dick was the main speaker at both occasions. There were over four hundred in attendance in Atlanta and about

200 in Macon. We met at First Baptist Church in Atlanta and were very pleased to have a greeting from the pastor. It was as though faith missions had a welcome into Southern Baptist territory!

It was also the 40th anniversary of Morning Glory Church in Tokyo. They asked us to return for the occasion. We left for Tokyo Sept. 20, less than two weeks after the Atlanta banquet. We felt the pressure, but knew that God would give us the strength, and His anointing. It was a blessing for both us and our son, Paul, to return to Japan to take part in the 40th anniversary celebration of our church. What had taken us 14 days by ship the first time, took ten hours by plane!

The first big occasion was a "welcome back" dinner with all those that had been with us in the beginning of Morning Glory

Church. It was held at a famous Chinese restaurant with over thirty people in attendance. What a royal welcome. We were overwhelmed! The next day was the anniversary service and Bernie was to speak. Having been away from Japan so long, and being unsure of his ability in Japanese, he asked Paul to interpret and he did a fine job.

Chapter 4

We were encouraged by the growth of the church in so many ways. Morning Glory's new building was beautiful and functional. But even more exciting was their emphasis on world missions as well as evangelism at home. They supported at least six couples on the foreign field, a number from their own membership. They had just planted one church and were in the process of beginning four others!

The church took good care of us; in fact, they spoiled us! They paid for our round trip fare, our lodging, and meals, and gave us

a beautiful vase. Part of the joy of our trip was visiting a beautiful Japanese SPA and a famous mountain where Japanese climbers practiced before going to the Swiss Alps. We had been somewhat apprehensive about the trip, but the Lord abundantly took care of us. We stayed well, we remembered more of the language than we thought, and Jeanette's new knees served her better than we expected, in spite of the crowds and climbing of stairs in using public transportation. God abundantly answered, and we were encouraged not only by what we saw, but what God did for us personally.

Jeanette's right knee did not responded to the replacement like the left one, in fact it deteriorated! She had an arthroscopy on May 20, 1991, by a specialist in Birmingham to make corrections or determine what should be done. Her knee improved somewhat, but still not completely.

Paul, Kathy, and boys had been living near us since Christmas. It was the first we'd had the joy of experiencing what it was really like to be grandparents especially because Jeremy was at a young age. Jeanette remembers making a cake for his first birthday with pink frosting. When she set it down in front of him, he exclaimed, "Yum, yum!" Another time, while grandpa was driving the car and Jeremy was standing in back of him, Bernie asked him, "Who do you love?" and he replied, "I love Mommy, I love Daddy, I love Grandpa, and I love Grandma and gum!" Jeanette especially enjoyed when Jeremy stood on his little stool and helped her with the dishes. He was always teasing by putting the silverware in the wrong places in the drawer. Jason's health had improved to the extent that they were able to return to Japan on September 16th.

Dave and Karen were settled in Minnesota in their new assignment as TEAM's Mission Hospital Coordinator. Bradley and Heather had adjusted well to the climate and culture.

PBA celebrated its 40th anniversary in September and invited us to be their guests. We hesitated in answering because of Jeanette's knee problem, but finally decided that I should go alone. I left September 5th and returned the 11th.

Family

We had the privilege of being with Dave, Karen, and children at Christmas. What a joyful time. We had an interesting telephone conversation with our family in Japan. They told of a visit Joshua had with a Japanese friend. When they asked him what he would say when he went to his friend's house, he said, "Gomen kudasai." So they asked him what that would mean in English to which he replied, "Hi you guys!" (It really means,

"Excuse me, please.") A little later we talked with Joshua on the phone. Jeanette was afraid he would not know who she was. So she explained he had two grandmas, Grandma DeBell and Grandma Holritz. Then she said, "I'm your Grandma Holritz," to which he replied emphatically, "I KNOW WHO YOU ARE!"

Several changes have taken place. Towards the end of last year, we began experiencing some problems with coping. Incidents that before were like ripples seemed like tidal waves! (I had just had my 70th birthday, and Jeanette jokingly said, "You must be having a belated midlife crisis!") So at the end of March, 1992, (ONE DAY AFTER THE 42nd ANNIVERSARY OF OUR SAILING TO JAPAN) we retired. We never dreamed there would be so much to do in retiring; Social Security, Medicare, and a host of other details. One by one, we completed them.

Since we left for Japan in 1950, we've had the joy of planting a church, co-founding a radio/TV ministry, thirteen years as its Stateside Representative and the past eleven years as TEAM's Southeast Representative. Many have been a definite part of all this as well as in the lives of our children, who continue as missionaries. We were greatly encouraged by the many letters, and cards that have come as well as overwhelmed by the surprise retirement banquet given by our home church, Killian Hill Baptist. Yes, we have been "workers together." THESE HAVE BEEN YEARS OF GOD'S MIRACLES!

Much wisdom was needed as there wasn't much room for a "mid-course correction." With our children being so far removed because of their ministries, and our health record as it was, we asked ourselves, how long should we wait before moving to a retirement village with the different levels of care. We'd rather not leave Georgia, but there was a dearth of good retirement homes in our price range. We wanted to continue being a witness, and use the gifts that God had given us.

Ministry in the U.S.

Since our retirement, we had been able to get some projects done around the house that we had put off a long time. That August, we visited our daughter and grandchildren in Minneapolis. Dave was away at the time. In October, we did something we've wanted to do ever since moving to Lilburn. We drove to northeast Georgia to view the fall colors. We were there at the very peak, and it was truly spectacular.

We also had visitors. Our son-in-law, Dave, after attending a seminar for doctors at the Billy Graham Conference Center in Ashville, NC, had a three day lay over before his next meeting in Dallas. We picked him up in Ashville, hoping to show him some beautiful country on our return, but it rained and was foggy the whole way back! The day we took Dave to the airport, we drove to Greenville, SC, to pick up our son, Paul, who had come to the States for three weeks of meetings representing a special project for personnel and finances in Japan. He also spent three days with us. We enjoyed the visits of Dave and Paul; in fact they were very providential. At this juncture of our lives, there were many decisions to make and their visits were very helpful.

Chapter Five
RETIREMENT YEARS: 1993 ~

Jeanette's December, 1992 foot surgery was rescheduled due to irregularity in her blood which the doctors thought could have been Myeloma. But after a series of tests, no cancer was found. So the date was rescheduled for January 27, 1993. This was to be total foot reconstructive surgery. They worked on all five toes, breaking bones, fusing joints, moving tendons, removing bunions, and putting in two three inch pins to hold things in place. It took four hours! The first six weeks were very painful. Because of severe swelling, Jeanette's foot needed to be elevated most of the time. In a cast to her knees and unable to put any weight on that foot, she was in a wheelchair. She had a removable brace that looked like an oversized ski boot, but still not allowed to put much weight on her foot. We were encouraged by the "get well" cards filling the top of the piano. Our church was wonderful; bringing meals, and helping with the house and lawn work.

At this point we want to remember Barry and Doris Waters (often referring to themselves as "the H2Os") and the blessing they always were to us. Every time we hear the words of Jesus, "This is My commandment that you love one another as I have loved you," we are reminded of Barry and Doris. Many are the times we were the recipients of their acts of love, and though their health was poor, they drew strength from the Lord, as they ministered. They truly are God's servants, always reaching out to others.

Dave went for two weeks of consultation to TEAM's hospital in Taiwan. Some interesting plans were also in the making for TEAM's medical missions worldwide involving Dave and Karen.

In July, we were thrilled to have our dear friends, the Iwasakis from Japan, plus their son, Akio (who was working on his doc-

rate at Purdue University) his wife, and four children to visit us. Karen had not seen the Iwasakis since 1966. In as much as she and Dave were at the mission's rep retreat, in Dayton, TN, Karen was able to drive down with Bradley and Heather to be with the Iwasakis. We had three wonderful days together- all twelve of us under one roof!

While we were together, we received a telephone call from Paul and Kathy in Japan with some very disturbing news. Kathy's health had been deteriorating. Doctors both in Japan and America recommended that they return to the States immediately. They needed housing and transportation, so we began looking for both hoping we would have something to present to them when they arrived August 11th. Again, we were glad for the house the

Chapter 5

Lord had provided for us when we came to Atlanta eleven years ago which made it possible for Paul, Kathy, and family to stay with us for six weeks until they moved into a house of their own. Then too, the four boys attended our church's school where they had been two years previously.

Karen had asked us several months earlier to come up to Minneapolis to help her while Dave had to be away in Mozambique for the mission, and we had agreed not knowing that we would have Paul, Kathy, and boys with us at that time. Paul and Kathy said they could take care of everything, so we went to Minneapolis in September. What a nice time we had. When we came back, we had to make a decision about Jeanette's right foot. In spite of her major right foot reconstruction in January, one of the toes was malfunctioning causing considerable pain. So on September 18, corrective surgery was done as an outpatient. We praise the Lord for good healing.

Kathy responded well to treatment and looked so much better. We can't help wishing it had not been necessary for them to have returned to the States, but thoroughly enjoyed having them so close in their new home –less than a mile away! We got to know the boys in a way that letters and telephone calls couldn't accomplish. We had a wonderful Christmas together.

On New Years day, 1994, Jeanette was walking around the house doing different chores when suddenly Jeremy said, "Grandma, you surely are walking fast." He had been praying for her everyday at mealtime and now he saw an answer to his prayers.

On January 2, we were at church early for the pre-service prayer meeting. Jeanette was with the ladies and Bernie with the men. As she stood to go, she caught her heel on the chair and fell to the concrete floor. When she tried to get up, she couldn't move! We called an ambulance to take her to the ER where we learned she had broken her hip! Thankfully her knee replacements were not injured nor were any other bones broken. It was a clean break, so they thought she would not need a hip replacement. On the third, she underwent surgery. Three screws were used to hold the bones together.

Two weeks after Jeanette's surgery, she found it to be far more painful than we had expected. She was in a wheelchair most of the time. Again our church was wonderful - bringing meals, helping with the housework, writing cards, calling on the phone, and visiting. We were especially indebted to Mary Frohm, who came for several weeks to do housework. Then too, Sally Leach and Georgia Housekneckt helped in other ways. We hadn't understood the Lord bringing Paul, Kathy and boys home, but they were such a blessing and encouragement when we needed them so very much.

After two months, it was evident that Jeanette's surgery wasn't successful and the doctor advised a total hip replacement. The second surgery (the seventh on that leg) was March 16. We rejoiced that her hip healed and she could walk mostly without a cane.

In March, Bernie accompanied Paul to Japan for a week to crate all their belongings for shipment back to the States. What a joy it was for him to meet those who had been led to Christ and see the work in which Paul and Kathy had been engaged for their two terms in Japan. They also were able to have a day in Tokyo to visit PBA and see the ministry they are carrying on.

In July, after TEAM's annual conference in Tennessee, Dave, Karen, Bradley, and Heather drove to Atlanta for a family reunion. It was a delightful visit. The children really enjoyed their time together to say nothing of the adults. The Drakes have been very busy in their new assignment as Medical Coordinator for the mission. Dave visited several of TEAM's hospitals, and in August, Karen joined him for two weeks at the hospital in Pakistan. They presented a hundred page procedural paper that will be a good tool for that field as well as others.

We continued to enjoy our time with Paul, Kathy, and the four boys, but our hearts were touched to see Kathy's various health problems. They found she was hypoglycemic. Further tests revealed she had a parasite (carried from Japan.) She severely reacted to all the medications, but that was brought under control, and she regained her appetite. Because of their circumstances, they took a two year leave of absence from their mission, which meant that Paul had to find employment.

It was very special to have the oldest son of our dear friends, the Iwasakis, here in Atlanta. His company had put him in charge of building a new factory just a few miles from where we live. Later, Dr. Hatori's daughter, Naomi, her husband, and their three children were with us. They were home on furlough from China.

We looked forward to a visit with the Drakes in Minneapolis at Christmas. (We hoped Jeanette wouldn't freeze too much!) As we rejoiced looking back at the great Gift of God's love to us, let's also look forward with anticipation for His return.

Fiftieth Anniversary

In February, 1995, our two children, Paul and Karen, sent announcements regarding our fiftieth wedding anniversary. The following are some of the details of what happened. Karen arrived on Thursday, March 23, 1995, to help Paul and Kathy with the final preparations. On Friday morning, the door bell rang and there stood Clarence, Bernie's only brother, his daughter, and granddaughter from California! It was a wonderful surprise and reunion!

On Saturday, Karen drove us to the church where we walked down the aisle to the strains of "Here Comes the Bride." Our pastor interviewed us regarding our wedding ceremony. When we responded negatively as to any of the bridal party being present, he asked, "How would you like to see two of them?" and pointed to the backdoor. Out walked Kris and Opal Solberg, from Seattle, Washington! Again, we were totally surprised.

The room had been beautifully decorated by our pastor's wife. There was an abundance of finger food, cake, and cookies, all

made by ladies of our church. As it was a "drop in" reception, there was no formal program as such, but background music by a violin duet. From time to time, Paul read letters from our various friends, and our grandsons, Nathan and Joshua, each played solos, Nathan on the clarinet, and Joshua on the violin. It was such a joy seeing so many that came to the reception. Dick Ryerson, the son of the lady who had been the pianist at our wedding came from South Carolina. Tyndale and Carolyn Langston, friends we had known over forty years, came from Kentucky. Tateo Iwasaki, the son of very dear friends from Japan, represented his parents and the church we co-founded in Tokyo, an MK who had grown up with our children in Japan, plus neighbors and friends from Atlanta, made up the many guests that came to celebrate with us.

Bernie shared his feelings with those at the reception, "We are what we are by the grace of God. He's given us friends who have prayed much for the Holritz family through the years. You share in this time of joy because you have had a part in bringing us to this hour, our thanks to you, for your faithfulness, and to our Heavenly Father, for His goodness to us."

Leaving the church, we glanced back once more at the beautiful decorations and thought of the happiness of the afternoon, hoping to capture in our memory a dream that we will never forget.

This song, sung at our wedding, has been a guide to us through the years of our married life:

>Sweetly, Lord, have we heard Thee calling,
>Come, Follow me!
>And we see where Thy footprints falling
>Lead us to Thee.
>
>Though they lead o'er the cold, dark mountains,
>Seeking His sheep;
>Or along by Siloam's fountains,
>Helping the weak:
>
>If they lead through the temple holy,
>Preaching the Word;
>Or in the homes of the poor and lowly,
>Serving the Lord;
>
>Then at last, when on high he calls us,
>Our Journey done,
>We will rest where the steps of Jesus
>End at His throne.

Chorus
Footprints of Jesus, that make the pathway glow;
We will follow the steps of Jesus where e'er they go.

Family

As we watched our grandson, Nathan, board the plane for Costa Rica for a ten day soccer/evangelistic tour, we prayed the Lord would use him, and that this would be a growing experience.

The Lord called Paul and Kathy to Tennessee Temple University in Chattanooga to head the Missions Department. They were seconded from their mission to the school, which means, they had to raise all their support again. Paul was pleased that his job description included taking students overseas as part of their training, putting him back into foreign missions.

While on a survey trip in Russia, on May 8th Dave was involved in a head on collision which injured his neck, broke four ribs, and dislocated a hip. Fortunately, he was not killed nor become a quadriplegic. During the flight back the only thing he had to brace his neck was a bath towel! When he arrived at the hospital, they discovered he didn't have a whip lash, but his number C2 vertebrae (just below the skull) was cracked and only millimeters from the spinal cord! During a very complicated surgery they fused the C1 & C2 vertebrae. When that was complete, they repaired his hip. We praise the Lord for His protection and Dave's miraculous recovery.

We finally located a retirement community that we believed would meet our needs for the future as well as our retirement budget. It was in Knoxville, TN, conveniently located to Paul and family in Chattanooga. (One and a half hours away.) This was dependent on the sale of our home in Lilburn. The main reason we felt we needed to be located in a three level facility now was that in order to enter, we had to be ambulatory and able to care for ourselves; starting with independent living, progressing (?) to assisted living, and finally the nursing home as it became necessary. Jeanette was doing well and only used a cane while walking out-of-doors. However, she was diagnosed as having spinal steno sis. We hoped this would be helped by exercise and cortisone. If not, it could mean a very serious back surgery to implant a steel plate. With her brittle bones, the outcome could be very uncertain.

Paul and Kathy were both busy; Paul teaching at Tennessee Temple, and Kathy teaching piano as well as pianist for Highland Park Baptist Church. In spite of her heavy schedule, we were thankful she was feeling well. The boys were all adjusting to their new location and friends. Our eleven year old Joshua was accepted into the Chattanooga Youth Symphony in the violin section. We attended his first concert on Dec. 5, 1995.

We rejoiced in Dave's recovery from his near fatal accident in Russia, and was back to his normal work load. Karen was busy with her teaching at Bethel University as well as working on her doctorate. We planned to be with the Drakes in Minnesota for Christmas. Paul and family planned to go also, but because the transmission on their car needed replacing, and being low on support, they were unable to make it.

Our Move to Knoxville, TN

Having been missionaries, we have moved most of our lives, from the time we set sail with our two babes in arms, to the land of Japan in 1950 until now. But somehow, we were in no way prepared for our recent move. We were able to sell our home in Lilburn, GA, and relocated in a retirement village in Knoxville, TN, on April 6, 1996, our 51 wedding anniversary.

How does one say goodbye to a pastor who has filled our hearts with the Living Word as well as dear Christian friends, who have

Retirement Years

faithfully ministered to our many physical afflictions and needs these past 15 years? To say it has been with painful hearts is an understatement! And yet, we find at the same time our lives are a paradox, for we felt at great peace at having made the move. As our children were deeply involved in their ministries, and we would not want to change that, we moved to an independent living facility with assisted living, and a nursing home facilities available as we had need. We wanted so much to stay in the Atlanta area, but after several years of looking, could not find a place that offered what this one does, and at this price. One thing we couldn't get over since moving to this community – everyone was old! We were definitely living in a mission field with perhaps the most difficult age of all people to reach.

It was a great comfort to us that two of our TEAM missionaries, the Rusty Sherwoods, and the Don Hokes, were living in this area as well as two couples from our Wheaton church, the Al Hamblys and the Howard McMillans. We were gradually getting settled. We were sure we had lost all our clothes hangers but wouldn't you know, they were in the last box opened!

In the process of applying for his Tennessee driver's license, a brown spot appeared in the central vision of Bernie's right eye. The ophthalmologist looked at it, and took him to the retinalogist. It was diagnosed as macular degeneration! A blood vessel had hemorrhaged, and needed to be cauterized by laser. That having been done, partial vision was restored.

Olympics

Our children had been extra busy. Paul moved into Olympic Village as one of the six interpreters for the Japanese Olympic team. Although the Olympics took a lot of time and energy, Paul felt it was very worthwhile as it gave him the opportunity of witnessing to people who would otherwise be unapproachable.

Chapter 5

Family - Jeanette

The Drakes were in Zimbabwe as a relief team where they had served so many years before returning to the States. Karen and the children returned August first, but Dave stayed until September first. Then Heather was diagnosed as a diabetic. That was a shocker, but she handled it well, and has kept it under control. They were happy to be home again. Karen said she felt sorry for Dave as three and a half months of mail awaited him plus all the car and house repairs that had piled up.

Thank the Lord, Bernie's eye made great improvement, which was a miracle, as we were told it could only get worse! In the meantime, Bernie had to have an endoscopy. There was inflammation, but the doctor said it could be taken care of by medication.

Something abnormal showed up on my physical, so the doctor suggested an endoscopy as well as a colonoscopy. I said, "I've always had endoscopies without an anesthetic so I thought I'd do the colonoscopy the same way. They had an IV in my arm in case I cried, 'uncle!' About half way through the test, I almost did, but I felt by then my reputation was at stake, so what else could I do?!" The nurses and doctors were all quite flattering. They never had a woman take the test without an anesthetic, and only one man who groaned the whole way through. "I just talked with them during the whole procedure. I'm not sure I would advise anyone else to do the same, but I will say I was awfully glad not to have to stick around for two hours in the recovery room."

All three families were together at Christmas. Thankfully, we just got under the wire for good tickets to Minneapolis, but we were much concerned for Paul's family, not only for the weather, as they drove straight through, but for their van, which they had been nursing along for sometime.

I had my second double knee replacements in March 1997. After five days in the hospital, I came home only to return for ten more days because of a blood clot in my left leg. I improved, and was walking, but was having trouble with my balance, which most likely was due to neuropathy in my feet. While I was recuperating from knee surgery, Dave, Karen, and children came for their first visit to our new home. It was a joy to show them around the area. The night before we were all to go to Chattanooga to visit Paul and family, a tornado ripped through their neighborhood doing an immense amount of damage. That area, which had never had a tornado before, had another just a month later which tore up some of their repairs.

While Paul was on a two week teaching module in Ecuador, he was privileged to take a trip to Palm Beach, where the five missionaries were martyred in 1956. Dayuma and her husband, the first Christians in the Auca tribe, escorted Paul to the site of the killing.

As reported earlier, Dave was almost killed in an auto accident in Russia about two years ago, and as a result, broke his neck. After surgery, and a time of healing, he was doing well. Then he was thrown from his bike re-injuring his neck. After two major surgeries, he made good strides in recovery with only a slight impairment which they hoped would clear up in a year or two. Although there had been much pain and suffering, it was a miracle God brought him through both ordeals which could have resulted in his being totally paralyzed.

Just after we moved to Knoxville, Bernie developed macular degeneration in his right eye. After laser treatment, his sight went from 20/200 to 20/30 – something the doctors did not expect. Six weeks ago, suddenly Bernie's left eye had a massive hemorrhage! Because of the residual blood in the eye, the doctor was unable to give a laser treatment. Bernie has virtually no central vision in that eye. Aside from a touch of the Lord, there wasn't much hope for any improvement.

With the move, getting settled, all these surgeries, and other happenings too numerous to mention, this was an emotionally draining year. But the Lord was gracious in giving us strength to carry on and not lose hope. His promise: "Though the outward man perishes, the inward man is renewed day by day." "We keep pressing toward the prize of the high calling of God in Christ Jesus."

At the recommendation of our orthopedic doctor in 1998, we went to a neurologist to find out why I was falling and having such a difficult time walking as well as shaking so much. It was a miserable feeling as well as wearing. His diagnosis was Parkinson's disease! We went through a period of adjusting medications. In the meantime, I fell and broke my right femur due to my imbalance. To add to the difficulty, my doctor was on vacation, and it was ten days before I could have surgery to mend my broken femur, then seven days more, before I came home from the hospital. My situation was made worse when I injured my back getting out of bed!

These incidents changed our whole summer. It wasn't until I got home that it dawned on us that we were supposed to be at the graduation of our grandson, Bradley, on May 29th. (Bradley graduated with honors and received the Principal's Award!) Soon bitterness crept into my heart, and I said with the Psalmist, "I'm cut off from before Thine eyes." How thankful I was to read the rest of Psalm 31:22, "Nevertheless Thou heardest the voice of my supplications when I cried unto Thee." And then the rest of verse 24, "Be of good courage and He shall strengthen your heart." "What a wonderful blessing my beloved husband was as he cared for me during those days. I believe the situation was harder on him than it was on me."

God graciously supplied our needs during that time. Our church, West Park Baptist, lovingly brought us meals for three weeks. Others prayed, sent gifts, and cards. We were even more confident, especially with our physical afflictions, that we were in the right place. A special blessing was not only the nursing home on the complex, but also the therapy department as well. It only took four minutes for Bernie to take me to therapy each day. We were also thankful that Paul and his family were nearby and visited us several times since my surgeries. To our delight as well as to others, the Holritz family was able to put on a concert at our retirement home on June 22; Paul, as emcee, Kathy, as accompanist, Bernie, as vocalist, Nathan, (17) on the piano and clarinet, Jason, (16) on the piano and organ, Joshua, (14) on the violin, and Jeremy, (10) on the trombone. I was so thankful I could attend in my wheelchair. What cheered us most was it gave our family the opportunity to be a witness both in word and song to our community.

Dave was in Zimbabwe and performed two successful surgeries in spite of his weak arms and hands due to his accidents. Heather (15) went on a mission outreach. An excerpt from one of her letters:

> "I'm saddened to hear that you are going through this trial, but I am happy to know this will help you grow stronger in your faith, and that is irreplaceable."

> Then Heather gave her own paraphrase of Isa. 40:30,31. "Grandmas grow weary, and grandpas may stumble and fall, but grandmas and grandpas that hope in the Lord WILL renew their strength. Grandmas will soar like eagles, and grandpas will run and not grow weary, grandmas will walk and not faint.

Chapter 5

"I hope this note will bring a smile to your face. Please NEVER forget God, the Almighty, has His loving arms around you.

"Keep those nurses in line or else I'll have to come to talk with them! Especially watch out for Grandpa, as he has a mischievous streak in him!!!"

Trying to keep up with the whereabouts of our children was almost impossible. In 1999, Dave and Karen were in South Africa, Zimbabwe, Cameroon, Benin, Ivory Coast, Gabon, Niger, Nigeria, as well as other states away from home. Paul and Kathy: Poland, Hungary, Austria, Switzerland, Ecuador, Japan as well as several States. Then our grandchildren are about the same, as they have traveled in missions, evangelistic singing groups, competition events, etc. Sometimes we wished life would be a bit quieter, but we would not want to keep our family from what the Lord has called them to do.

Conversely, the mom and dad, grandma and grandpa of this family (because of health) led a far different life style. Bernie had macular degeneration and lost most of the sight in his left eye, but he had 20/20 vision in the right. A year ago, I was diagnosed with Parkinson's disease. I had fallen three times resulting in a broken femur, and later a surgery to repair it. Because of my spinal steno sis, my back surgeon hoped to at least be able to get me on my feet again. The surgery was scheduled for June 11, 1999.

This was a difficult year, but should we wonder about such adversity when we are warned by Peter, "not to consider it strange concerning the fiery trial which is to try us as though some strange thing happened unto us." Thank God, He never forsakes His own, and we have found through it all, His blessings out weigh the trials. He gave us many good friends to pray for us, and help along the way. Not long ago, some of these friends heard that I needed a four wheel walker. They bought one of such quality I called it my "Cadillac," however, when our youngest grandson, Jeremy, loaded it with all his toys and stuffed animals; it was his "pick-up truck." (Jeremy was always the first to run out to the car when we visited them and say, "Hi Grandma. Can I help you; can I help you?")

On June 11, I had back surgery with the verdict that I had damaged nerves, and would never walk again without special shoes and metal braces. When I saw the clumsy shoes and braces, I decided to try some rigid exercises first. Thankfully, as the result of therapy, I was able to walk with a walker or cane without braces. At the time of back surgery, I was taken off Parkinson's medication and have never used it again. A miracle! I no longer carry the stigma of Parkinson's disease.

Because I fell and broke my femur last year, we had to cancel our trip to Minneapolis for Bradley's graduation, but the Drakes "went to work on the airlines" and got our tickets extended so that we could be with them for Thanksgiving. We were grateful that I was able to make the trip and to enter into all the family's activities. It was always a joy to be with our children and grandchildren, and to see their development. The four Holritz boys are all musical, and each plays a different instrument. Joshua, our fifteen year old, was chosen from the Youth Symphony as a soloist for a violin concerto with the Chattanooga Symphony! Dave and Karen's Bradley, is a computer aficionado, and also operates the sound system for their church. Their Heather has won several medals for her soccer playing, and her heart's desire is to become a missionary doctor like her father. (Brad and Heather are both diabetic, but thankfully, so far it has not affected any of their vital organs.) Most of all, we are thankful that each of our children and grandchildren have a personal relationship with our Lord Jesus.

Chapter 5

Story Telling with Our Grandchildren - Bernie

Because of our grandchildren growing up on the mission field, we missed their younger years, but we were thankful Karen reported the doings of Brad and Heather. Each of our grandchildren from both families sent us birthday cards which they had made as well as wrote us letters on occasion.

That which especially stands out about Brad was his love for imitating any and all motorized vehicles. (They had to watch him in relationship to their car. When he was a year and seven months, he found the car keys and inserted them in the ignition!) Regarding Heather, the missionaries remarked of her charm as a little blond girl.

We tried in every way to keep in touch with our grandchildren by sending gifts and taped children's programs from the Moody station. Bradley would listen to the tapes we sent to Dave and Karen over and over and would try to repeat in his own words what he had heard. Then Karen asked that we not only send tapes to Dave and herself, but personal tapes to Brad and Heather. That was the beginning of our story telling tapes to all our grandchildren – mostly about wild life around our area. Doing this was fun for us as well. The story they all seemed most interested in was about a tiny flying squirrel that got into our attic. (Of course we made the tapes as mysterious as possible.) The first thing that each of the grandchildren asked when they arrived at our home was," Tell us about that flying squirrel!"

Family picture - Jeanette

We met together in July 2001, at Paul and Kathy's home in PA. The picture is a record of that occasion. It was not easy to get the family together as the children grew older. We were thankful to have everyone there even though some came late and others left

early. The girl standing just behind Bernie is Nate's wife, Amber. They announced at that time that we would become great grandparents near the end of January! That was hard to fathom! But we were all excited.

Anniversaries

This was a special year. The anniversary dates for Morning Glory Church were to be October 7, and October 8th for Pacific Broadcasting Association, making it easier for us to attend both to which we were invited. However, Jeanette's health did not allow such strenuous travel. So Bernie went and our son, Paul, arranged his schedule in order to join him.

In the meantime, Bernie was working with Art Seely (one of the other cofounders of PBA) to prepare a history of PBA's ministry. It was a blessing to review all that had happened through the years and how the Lord's Hand had directed even in stops that occurred along the way. The two main goals that were set up at the beginning: nation- wide coverage by radio and TV, and to be fully indigenous both in personnel and finances, had become a reality. We were reminded of the verse, "The Lord has done great things for us whereof we are glad." Psa. 126:2.

Chapter 5

Morning Glory Church's 50TH Anniversary

The activities began Saturday evening, Oct. 6th, with a banquet at a nearby Chinese restaurant primarily for about 50 of the long

time members. It was the first for me to meet and get acquainted with the present pastor, Rev Toshio Gotoh and his wife, Toshiko. What a moving experience to look at the group and recall incidents in the lives of each of them. The next day, Sunday, the

church was filled with more than 200 in attendance. Bernie was privileged to bring the morning message using the Apostle Paul's words in I Cor. 1:1-3 to greeting and encourage the church. Our son, Paul, was Bernie's interpreter. In the afternoon, Rev. Junji Hatori, former pastor, spoke followed by the presentation of gifts to the founders and early leaders who were present. Morning Glory Church had "mothered" three churches that are completely independent. There were two, soon to be four, from the church who were in full time missions overseas. In addition, they have partial support for about 20 other missionaries.

October 8th, Pacific Broadcasting Association's 50th Anniversary – Bernie

This was a full hour program in a beautiful banquet hall with over 400 present. These were people who supported PBA, representatives of radio and television stations that carried our programs, board members and staff. It was an inspiring program

which included a series of film clips from the beginning to the present in which we witnessed the growth from one weekly radio program until today there are five, a ten, and a fifteen minute daily radio program giving nation wide coverage, plus a thirty minute weekly TV program on ten stations as well as a daily broadcast over Trans World Radio from Guam. I was given a

Chapter 5

brief time to reminisce using our son, Paul, as my interpreter. Then Art Seely and I were presented with gifts of appreciation. At that time, we made a presentation to PBA of $3,500 which came from donors in the U.S. There is a bonding that takes place when working together to begin a ministry. Such is the case with Akira Hatori, Art Seely, and myself. It was work, sweat, and tears mingled with a lot prayer. I thank God for those two wonderful brothers.

October 25th, BERNIE'S 80th Birthday

Unbeknown to me, Jeanette, Karen, and Paul, sent out a letter suggesting a card shower. It was a "cloud burst!" What a surprise when Deana Forkum showed up at the door with a birthday

cake and a basket full of cards! It was overwhelming, a word I've used several times this month. There were over 200 cards. It took three days to open and read them in the midst of a lot of smiles and tears. How wonderful to have so many caring friends.

My brother, Clarence, in CA, hadn't been well. So the day after Thanksgiving, I went to see him and the Lord greatly blessed the time. The "icing on the cake" was that his youngest son, Kelly,

Retirement Years

accepted the Lord as his personal Savior. It was difficult to leave Clarence, Pat, his wife, and Kelly.

Jeanette's health hasn't changed much, but her spirits were up and she was coping very well. We stayed home for Christmas, but were looking forward to Paul, Kathy, and boys visiting us for about three days. Because of all the traveling Dave had been doing, and the need for Karen to put the finishing touches on her doctoral dissertation, they did not come.

It was 2002, and we felt like we had traveled around the world as we followed our family in prayer – Paul, two weeks in Bangladesh, Karen, one month in Korea and Japan, Dave, six weeks in various parts of Africa, and it was not over yet! Our granddaughter, Heather, left for Kenya for six months, and about the same time Paul left again, this time for two weeks in Egypt. We thank God for His watch care over all their travel in the past, and pray for His blessing and safe keeping in the future.

We had some new experiences in our retirement community as the Lord opened avenues of service for which we praise Him. I had the opportunity of singing again. What a blessing it was to use the talent the Lord had given me even at 81! I sang with the choir that puts on a concert twice a year and was privileged to be one of the soloists. Once a month, I sang and led the singing at chapel. It was the means of being a witness for Christ.

Though our family had been out of the country, we were thankful they could be in the U.S. for Christmas. Much to our sorrow, we had to cancel our plans to be with the Drakes, but we had the joy of being with Paul and his family.

Another highlight was working with Pacific Garden Mission to get their program in Japanese on the air. In the process, they asked for my life story which was aired on "Unshackled" the week of January 19, 2003.

Chapter 5

Jeanette had two falls that year. It was for that reason we had to cancel our flight to Minneapolis at Christmas. With aid of a cortisone shot, she was able to weather the fractured pelvis fairly well, but the second fall wasn't so easy. From the bone scan, we learned that there were two compressed vertebra: one new, and the other old. The pain had been intense, and medication didn't seem to phase it. The pain lessened when she laid down, and thankfully slept well at night. Then it was Bernie's turn when he was rushed to the hospital with a heart attack, resulting in an implantation of a stent. A second trip to the hospital brought Karen from Minneapolis, and Paul from Winston-Salem both with a deep concern that it was time for their mother and father to be located near one of them.

With neither of us able to do any of the packing, Karen and her daughter, Heather, as well as Paul and Kathy worked hard on packing and loading the U haul truck. On April 15, we were on our way to Winston-Salem, NC, with all our earthly belongings. To God be the glory for a safe trip, and three days of beautiful weather for loading and unloading. We settled into Creekside Retirement Center just minutes from Paul and Kathy. Thank the Lord we slowly regained our strength.

Paul was Executive Vice President of Piedmont Baptist College in Winston-Salem, NC, and Kathy was Assistant Director of Admissions. It was wonderful to see the way the Lord used their gifts and talents. We enjoyed living near them and our grandson, Jeremy, enabling us to attend church together, and have other activities during the week. Nathan, Amber, and our only great grandson, Austen, live in Chattanooga as do Jason and Theresa. Joshua is still in NY serving an internship with his violin professor. The entire Holritz family planned to be together at Christmas, but we were not sure whether the Drakes could come.

Retirement Years

2004

We attended a momentous occasion – the graduation ceremony of our daughter, Karen, on May 17, 2004, in which she was presented her Doctor of Philosophy in Education Policy and Administration with a concentration in Comparative and International

Development Education from the University of Minnesota. We were thankful for Dave who supported Karen so sacrificially through these years of arduous study. Paul and Kathy were also with us, so together with our grandchildren, Brad and Heather, it was a special time for us all.

At the retirement home in Winston-Salem, Jeanette was in a wheelchair or with a walker so I have had little time for public ministry. However, we felt the Lord had burdened our hearts for our fellow residents at Creekside where the medium age was 82. Because of this, we often heard a fire truck and an ambulance at the entrance of our building to rush someone to the hospital. A few months ago, after I had visited one of the residents in the hospital almost on a daily basis, he accepted the Lord as his Savior. His wife and relatives were overjoyed as they had been praying for him for years. At the same time, I was ministering to another man in the hospital. Eventually both men died within a day of each other, and I was asked to conduct a memorial service for each man on the same day! Since that time, Jeanette has been trying to fill the void in both widows' lives, one of whom had no children. After all of this, several of the residents asked if Bernie would conduct Sunday morning worship services.

Last, but not least, we cannot resist showing you a picture of our only great grandson. He is the son of Nathan and Amber, Paul and Kathy's oldest son.

We said goodbye to our Minnesota family after three wonderful days together at Christmas. But it wasn't an easy time for them getting here! Some came by car and some by plane, but all were held up by the snowstorm in Ohio. The group from Minnesota included not only Dave, Karen, Heather, and Bradley, but also three Zimbabweans, whom the Drakes were helping to sponsor through college. The five young people spent the nights with Paul, Kathy, Joshua, and Jeremy, while Dave and Karen stayed with us. Nathan, Amber, and Austen were with Amber's parents in Ashville, NC, while Jason and Theresa were to be with her parents in IN, but spent three nights in Cincinnati airport finally arriving early Saturday morning the 24th – minus their luggage which they finally recovered. They all returned safely to their homes without the problem of snow they encountered on the way down here.

In 2005, Karen left for Africa for two weeks to help set up a nursing school in Uganda. Dave was feeling better and making plans for a trip to South Africa sometime in early spring. Paul and Kathy were at Piedmont Baptist College where many exciting events were taking place. All the grandchildren were either working or at school.

At Creekside Retirement Home, I had been alternating with two other speakers at the Sunday Vesper Services, as well as counseling with individuals. As for our health, I had lost fifteen pounds and the doctor was taking tests to find out the reason. Jeanette continued using her wheelchair, but had many other medical problems.

This was a momentous year for the Holritzes. Jeanette celebrated her 80th birthday on July 30. She received almost 200 cards, most with long notes recalling times past. Oh what fun she had opening those cards! In addition, she had the surprise of her life by the visit of her three sisters (whom she had not seen for ten years) – all initiated by Paul and Kathy and joined by Dave and Karen in financing their trip. Jeanette's sisters commented on the blessing it was to see a loving family caring for one another.

Chapter 5

We celebrated our 60th wedding anniversary on April 6th. Paul called us that morning saying he would be bringing a package to our door. It turned out to be Karen from Minnesota! These 60 years were not without trials, but we thanked the Lord for the joy of being together.

Karen was delighted to have Dave join her for the last part of her visit to Uganda. Bradley continued his work with a computer company for which he travels a great deal. Heather was taking her senior year with courses on line from Liberty College.

We received word that Paul had passed his comprehensive exam for his doctoral studies which will better qualify him for the position he held at Piedmont Baptist College. Kathy stood by him in these busy days. Nathan and Amber have their own photography business. They have given us our only great grandchildren, Austen three and a half years, and Addison, just six months old. We saw Addison for the first time on Jeannette's birthday. Jason and

Theresa returned from a mission trip to Brazil. Jason returned early because of his responsibility at work, and preparation for his second year at seminary. Joshua won the violin concerto contest in the music camp in London and was chosen as the soloist with the camp orchestra for their final performance. (An interesting side light—Joshua's violin teacher loaned him his ninety thousand dollar violin to take with him to London!) Jeremy, our youngest grandson, attends NC School of Arts in order to finish his high school as well as for study in classical guitar.

"You are the movingest people I've ever met!" This was probably the truth as we have moved more than twenty times in our married life. At the request of our son and daughter, we moved from an independent living facility in NC to an assisted living facility in MN the middle of October, 2005.

We had a very nice Christmas with Dave, Karen, Bradley, and Heather, plus two of Dave's sisters and the three Zimbabweans whom they helped support through college. Our children continued their travels: Paul and Kathy returned just before Christmas from three weeks of ministry in Burma, and Karen left for three week in Uganda. Jeanette continued her life in a wheelchair due to her neuropathy, and fouled up knees that are irreparable. She loves to write and is determined to put notes on all the newsletters as much as possible.

Karen and Dave moved us up to Minneapolis last October, 2005, to be near them, but then this year, on September first, Karen left for a nine months assignment in Uganda and Dave will join her shortly. We have tried to adjust to living in this big city where our doctors are not nearby, and it would not be unusual to travel an hour to a hospital or a doctor's appointment. In relation to our travel, we asked for prayer for Bernie's eye sight. The retinalogist ran tests on the good eye to see if there were signs of change, but thankfully there were none.

2007

We were not fond of giving "organ recitals" (health reports). But our lives were and are greatly affected by our health these days. For a long time, Jeanette had suffered a great deal from what was thought to be Parkinson's disease, but was finally diagnosed as "Familial Tremor." (That means the tremor is inherited.) The shaking has become so severe that it is difficult for her to hold anything or feed herself. It is hard for me to see her deteriorate and not be able to do anything about it.

It has been a long time since we made a family picture. There were 18 of us, including two guests as we gathered at the Drake's house for Christmas of 2007. We had three wonderful days together celebrating the birth of our Lord Jesus, talking, playing games, singing, and thanks to Nate and Amber, taking pictures. Our family came to MN from NC, TN, and CA. Those from TN and NC drove and had trouble with snow. It took about twenty

hours each way! It was wonderful to have Christmas with children around again, especially when it is our own great grandchildren (Nate and Amber's 5 and 3 year olds.) Another surprise was the announcement of Bradley's engagement to Megan Sherman. They plan a May wedding.

After the reunion, everyone scattered. Karen had just a few days to prepare for her trip to Uganda where she will be for the month of January, 2008. She accompanied 24 nursing students who took part in a special training program. Dave stayed home because of some other activities including the care of Heather, who had major foot surgery. Paul and Kathy returned to NC, where Paul continued to work on his dissertation and Kathy her school responsibilities. (Before coming to the reunion, Joshua had just returned from Vienna where he had participated in some concerts with his school's string quartette, as well as played in the Vienna Symphony.) Nate, Amber, and children returned to their photography business in Chattanooga; Jason and Theresa to the schools where they work.

On the home front, they were still unable to help Jeanette's Familial Tremor. I had trouble with my right knee. After an arthroscopy, a hematoma developed which took six weeks to heal and then he was walking well.

On April 6, 2008, we celebrated our 63rd wedding anniversary. The facility where we live provided a private room for Dave, Karen, Jeanette, and Bernie with flowers, a decorated cake, and of course a good meal. While eating, calls came from family members making it a delightful time.

We had lived in Farmstead, an assisted living facility in Minneapolis, for almost two and a half years. Little by little, Jeanette needed more help for her daily living. The early part of March, 2009, she fell resulting in two crushed vertebra, five days in the hospital, and another five days in rehabilitation. At the same time, I had another episode with my heart that put me in the hospital four days.

In discussing the new situation with the folks at Farmstead, and as a family, it was decided that Jeanette should go into a health care facility. Miraculously, there was an opening with the same organization as Farmstead. So Jeanette moved March the 14th and Bernie moved into an independent living facility on the same grounds on the 24th. She has a private room and Bernie has a one bedroom apartment. It was a seven minute walk from Bernie's door to Jeanette's. Dave, Karen, Heather, and a couple of their friends moved us. Karen and Heather put Bernie's apartment in order and some furniture and pictures in Jeanette's room.

This was very difficult for both of us and will take awhile to get used to. Dr. Jeremiah would call this "A Bend in the Road." For Jeanette, it was a different kind of facility with occupants that are not as healthy mentally or physically as they were at Farmstead. So the combination of our not living together and the adjustment to these conditions are especially hard for her. The staff keeps everything clean. Jeanette enjoys the physical therapy and the extra time for personal Bible study. Bernie eats supper with

Jeanette and spends the evenings, and we talk often on the phone which takes some of the sharpness out of the separation.

Family news!

Our grandson, Bradley Drake, married Megan Sherman on May 2nd. (They met when Megan was in Uganda as student from Bethel Univ. and Bradley was visiting his folks for Christmas.) The wedding was a beautiful and Christ honoring occasion.

In October, I felt like an old battleship being "taken out of mothballs" and "re-commissioned." Town East Baptist Church in San Antonio, Texas, where I had been their first mission conference

speaker, was having their 47th mission conference, asked if I could join them to sing and to speak! Jeanette was being well cared for and felt at ease about my going. I was hosted by Bro. Joe and Doris West. It was absolutely a wonderful conference, as the Spirit of the Lord was so evident in all of the services.

God has been teaching us many lessons lately. A few weeks ago, I went shopping for some groceries. When checking out, I reached for my wallet, and to my horror, it wasn't there! I put all my groceries back in the cart and asked Customer Service to hold them while I went back to my apartment to get my wallet. Suddenly I remembered I could get cash from the branch bank. So I drew out what I thought was enough, got my cart, and went through the line again. But when the cashier had checked all my groceries, I was almost $17 short! I started eliminating what I could get along without, but was still a couple of dollars short. I started to pick another item when the lady behind me said, "Never mind, I'll make up the difference." I thanked her, but said she didn't need to do that as I could do without those items. But she insisted and paid the bill. When I finished bagging my groceries, the cashier said, "Don't forget these items!" The lady had paid for all the items I had eliminated! I thanked her again. Then she put a box of cookies into my bag and said, "This is from me." What an example of the Scripture, "My God shall supply all your needs according to His riches in glory by Christ Jesus."

We had a wonderful Christmas with Dave, Karen, Bradley, Megan, Heather, and her boy friend as we celebrated the birth of our Savior. We ate, talked, opened packages, and watched a video. In between all of this, we had telephone calls from friends and the rest of our family.

Karen, and a couple of her colleagues, plus thirty of her students, left for Uganda for five weeks of study on January first. Paul planned to defend his dissertation by the end of January, 2009. What a long ordeal that had been! Joshua visited us the end of January when he came to audition for enrollment in the University of Minnesota's School of Music.

In May, when Paul received his PhD from Regent University in Norfolk, VA, he said, "Now, Mom and Dad, God has given you a paradox – (a pair of docs.)" Karen got hers a few years ago. No credit to us – I had graduated from college, but because of the

Retirement Years

births of our children, Jeanette only completed two years. Shortly after graduation, Paul left for Romania, where he taught a module to some pastors, and spoke in several churches. In July, he went to Japan, and then to an undisclosed location to speak to another group of pastors. While Paul was in Romania, Kathy was able to visit her mother in Seattle, who celebrated her 80th birthday. At the same time, Dave and Karen left for five weeks in Uganda where Karen set up a Master's Degree program in the nursing school she helped to establish. This school serves the purpose of taking her students from Bethel University to see missionary work, as well as observe a foreign culture, in case the Lord should lead any of them in that direction.

We are thankful that our children are involved in worldwide ministries. We dedicated them to serve the Lord , and grateful for those who have prayed for them all these years, as well as those who continue to pray for our grandchildren and great grandchildren.

Jeanette kept herself busy by giving our tracts, placing mail orders, memorizing a number of Psalms, including her favorite, the 34th, and other select passages. The most difficult part for Jeanette was that she was cognitive, and yet in the dining room, there probably weren't more that two people with whom she could carry on a conversation. There are some who even shout at times.

What we really miss is the patter of little feet. In most other cities where we have lived, the Lord had blessed us with young couples who brought their children while helping in other ways. We still carry on correspondence with them, but they are so far away, just as are our great grandchildren, but we are cheered by the thought that we are here by God's appointment.

Celebrations

Surprise! Surprise! – We all love surprises. It was 2010, Jeanette's 85 birthday and our 65 wedding anniversary. I drove

her to Dave and Karen's where she was told there would be a surprise awaiting. She was in her wheelchair and we put her on the back patio with her eyes closed. When we told her to open her eyes there stood our entire family, with the exception of Bradley and Megan. She was overwhelmed!

After supper we gathered in the dining room where they presented her with two beautifully decorated note books filled with loving remembrances from our many friends. We were all given

party hats and whistles and a large cake with "Happy 85th Birthday" was brought in. Because Paul's birthday was just a few days off, they had another cake for him as well. It was an occasion never to be forgotten!

Chapter 5

Jeanette's graduation

We were privileged to have Christmas and New Years with the Drakes. Because the family had been together earlier in the year there was no one from out of town that came. The next few weeks of 2011 progressed as usual with my visits to Jeanette on a daily basis. We worked on the editing of our memoirs. We were within eight pages of completing them when one day Jeanette starting developing a deep cough and by Friday, March 4th, Vicky, the house nurse, had an X-Ray taken which showed pneumonia in both lungs and prescribed an antibiotic to fight it. Monday afternoon I went as usual to visit Jeanette. I was fine until about 8 when I began feeling sick and started running a temperature.

On Tuesday I visited the doctor and an X-Ray revealed congestion in the right lung. He sent me home to bed with some antibiotics. I felt badly not being able to get over to see Jeanette, but we talked several times a day by phone. Dave and Karen had planned their vacation in the Caribbean several months before. On Friday the doctor told them that Jeanette was out of danger and that they should go. So they left on Saturday morning. But on Sunday morning Jeanette took a turn for the worst and at 2 a.m. Monday I was called saying they were sending Jeanette to the hospital in an ambulance!

Not being able to drive at night I called Heather and she came as soon as she could. When we arrived at the ER the doctor met us saying he didn't think she would make it till day break! The hospital had already called Karen's cell phone to inform her not knowing she was in the Caribbean. She said they would take the next flight back. The doctor asked me what he should do. I told him "Nothing heroic. Just fight the disease."

As I watched the dials and saw how high her pulse rate was (185 bpm) I knew she couldn't keep that rate for long. They put her on a high dosage of antibiotics intravenously, and an oxygen mask on her face. Little by little her oxygen level went up and her heart rate went down. All the family was notified and as many as could came.

We all took turns staying with her. She began to rally and was very conversant. Paul told of the wonderful time he had with her as he read and she quoted lengthy passages from the Psalms including her favorite - the 34th. She was doing quite well until Thursday when she began to loose ground. As I was alone with her, she asked, "Am I going to live or am going to die?" I said, "Which do you want to do?" She said, "I want to live." I said, "We are doing all we can to make that possible." Later as Nathan and I were with her she said to Nate, "I'm going to die. Please take good care of Grandpa." One of the amazing things that happened was about an hour before the Lord called her, the Seniors' Pastor from Calvary Church where I attend came by to see her and they talk together and had prayer.

Several of us were with Jeanette holding her hand and telling her we loved her as she gradually stopped breathing. At five minutes to four Sunday afternoon March 20th, just seventeen days before our sixty-sixth wedding anniversary, the Lord called my dear Honey home to be with Him! She had fought a good fight; she kept the faith; the battle was over. She is free of pain and all the maladies and has a new body. Now she sees "Him whom having not seen, she loved." Praise the Lord for what He has made possible through Jesus Christ,

In closing, I want to pay tribute to my dear Honey. Life, particularly in her younger days, was never easy. She had to strive for everything she had. When she came to know Jesus as her personal Savior, life took on new meaning and new hope. After graduating from high school, as you have read her story, she sensed the call of the Lord to full surrender. She answered that call and never turned back. From the time I first saw her and heard her testimony I knew she was to be my life partner. There were three things that I saw then and that was true of her life to the last day: she loved the word of God; she loved the Lord Jesus; and she loved souls. She was never afraid to take a stand for Jesus and was always ready to testify of Him.

Another quality that I greatly admired was her hatred for sin. I'm sure that the home life from whence she came had a great deal to do with it. She saw where that kind of life would lead and she did not want anything with it to do. If we were watching a video and a promiscuous scene came on the screen, she would say, "I don't want to watch that video." One time she asked Joyce Betz to make a plaque to go over our TV, in her beautiful script, of Psalms 101:3, " I will set no wicked thing before mine eyes...." If someone told a shady joke, she didn't hesitate to mention that such jokes were inappropriate for a Christian.

One day as we were doing some reminiscing, I thought back upon all the different places we had live (I counted 30! Some for a long time some for a very short time.) Wherever we were, she made a beautiful home for us. She had a knack of taking something that wasn't very homey and converting it into something very attractive.

Few people knew that her first name was Dora, which means "gift." I called her, "My Theodora" which means "gift of God." Truly, she was God's gift to me. "Thank you Lord for my dear Theodora."

Some travels

I had not seen my California relatives in about ten years and each time we had visited them before, it was always on the run and never took the time to really visit. So in September I spent five days with the Holritz clan in the Los Angeles area and five days with my grandson, Bradley Drake, and his wife in San Francisco. It was a wonderful time of re-connecting with loved ones.

PBA was celebrating its 60th anniversary and they asked Art Seely and me to come, if health permitted. Right up to the last I

was not sure if Art could make it as his health was not good. Dr. Hatori at 91 wasn't well either, but both men seemed to revive and we had a wonderful time together. There was a reunion first for all the "old boys" met together to reminisce. The formal anniversary was on October 7.

Morning Glory Church was celebrating its 61st anniversary and postponed their celebration until I got there. I spoke to the

church on Sunday, October 2nd. It was wonderful to meet with them again, but sad to note the absence of so many who had changed their address to heaven. Of course to meet together with the Iwasaki family was very special. How wonderful to sense that same deep love for one another that had not changed.

A week after returning to the States I participated in the annual mission conference in San Antonio, TX. It is always a time of special blessing. One of those was to be in the conference with Paul. This was our second time to be together in a conference.

I returned home in time to celebrate my 90th birthday with family.

In conclusion it is our (yes, Jeanette's too) prayer that this record of God's miracles in our lives has been a blessing and encouragement to your walk with the Lord; that you will see His faithfulness and love for His children. We thank the Lord for the many faithful partners who have supported our family prayerfully and financially these many years. As the song writer penned, "Jesus led me (us) all the way". To Him be all the praise and glory. Amen!

To contact the author:

Bernie Holritz
3120 Lake Johanna Blvd #106
Arden Hills, MN 55112-7953
651-697-6670
763-516-7126 (cell)